Varieties of
Progressivism
in America

This book is a publication
of the Hoover Institution's

Initiative on
American Individualism
and Values

The Hoover Institution
gratefully acknowledges

MR. AND MRS. CLAYTON W. FRYE JR.

for their generous support
of this book project.

VARIETIES OF
Progressivism
IN AMERICA

Edited by

**PETER
BERKOWITZ**

Contributors

DAVID COLE

THOMAS BYRNE EDSALL

FRANKLIN FOER

WILLIAM A. GALSTON

JEFFREY C. ISAAC

RUY TEIXEIRA

HOOVER
INSTITUTION
PRESS
Stanford University
Stanford, California

www.hoover.org

Hoover Institution Press Publication No. 534

First printing, 2004
11 10 09 08 07 06 05 04   9 8 7 6 5 4 3 2 1

Manufactured in the United States of America

The paper used in this publication meets the minimum requirements
of the American National Standard for Information Sciences—
Permanence of Paper for Printed Library Materials, ANSI Z39.48-1992. ∞

Library of Congress Cataloging-in-Publication Data

Varieties of progressivism in America / edited by Peter Berkowitz.
        p.   cm. — (Hoover Institution Press publication series ; 534)
    Includes bibliographical references and index.
    ISBN 0-8179-4582-2
    1. Democratic Party (U.S.)   2. Progressivism (United States politics)
I. Berkowitz, Peter, 1959–   II. Series: Hoover Institution publication ; 534.
JK2316.V37   2004
324.2736—dc22   2004018471

CONTENTS

Peter Berkowitz teaches at George Mason University School of Law and is a fellow at the Hoover Institution, Stanford University. He is a founding codirector of the Jerusalem Program on Constitutional Government and served as a senior consultant to the President's Council on Bioethics. He is the author of *Virtue and the Making of Modern Liberalism* (1999) and *Nietzsche: The Ethics of an Immoralist* (1995), as well as editor of *Never a Matter of Indifference: Sustaining Virtue in a Free Republic* (2003) and of the companion to this volume, *Varieties of Conservatism in America* (2004). He has written on a variety of topics for a variety of publications.

David Cole is a professor at Georgetown University Law Center, volunteer staff attorney for the Center for Constitutional Rights, legal affairs correspondent for *The Nation*, and a commentator on NPR's *All Things Considered*. He is author, most recently, of *Enemy Aliens: Double Standards and Constitutional Freedoms in the War on Terrorism* (2003).

Thomas Byrne Edsall is a national political reporter for the *Wash-*

ington Post. He is the author of *The New Politics of Inequality* (1984), *Power and Money* (1988), and *Chain Reaction* (1992). He is also the winner of the Carey McWilliams Award of the American Political Science Association.

Franklin Foer is an associate editor at the *New Republic* and a contributing editor at *New York Magazine*. He is the author of *How Soccer Explains the World: An Unlikely Theory of Globalization* (2004).

William A. Galston is Saul Stern Professor at the School of Public Policy, University of Maryland; director of the Institute for Philosophy and Public Policy; and founding director of CIRCLE: The Center for Information and Research on Civic Learning and Engagement. From 1993 until 1995, he served as Deputy Assistant for Domestic Policy to President Clinton. He is the author of numerous books and articles, including *Liberal Pluralism* (2002) and *The Practice of Liberal Pluralism* (2004).

Jeffrey C. Isaac is James H. Rudy Professor and chair of the Department of Political Science at Indiana University. He is also the director of the Center for the Study of Democracy. His books include *The Poverty of Progressivism: The Future of American Democracy in a Time of Liberal Decline* (2003); *Democracy in Dark Times* (1998); *Arendt, Camus and Modern Rebellion* (1992); and *Power and Marxist Theory* (1987). He also writes regularly for *Dissent* magazine, on whose editorial board he serves.

Ruy Teixeira is a senior fellow at both the Center for American Progress and The Century Foundation. He is the author of five books; hundreds of articles, both scholarly and popular; a weekly online column, "Public Opinion Watch"; and a daily weblog, "Donkey Rising." His latest book is *The Emerging Democratic Majority* (2002), written with John Judis.

ACKNOWLEDGMENTS

This book and its companion volume, *Varieties of Conservatism in America*, appear under the auspices of the Hoover Institution's Initiative on American Individualism and Values. Both volumes are animated by the conviction that it is advantageous, particularly at this moment of high partisan passion in the United States, to explore the inclinations, opinions, and ideas that inform partisan differences, as well as the principles that partisans in America share. The volumes, and the conviction that animates them, have enjoyed the generous support of Hoover Institution director John Raisian and deputy director David Brady.

Peter Berkowitz
Washington, D.C.

INTRODUCTION

Peter Berkowitz

IT HAS BECOME CUSTOMARY in the United States to refer to the left of center in American politics as "liberal." This, however, is misleading because a liberal in the large sense, as Judith Shklar stressed, seeks, in the first place, "to secure the political conditions that are necessary for the exercise of personal freedom"[1]—a description that also fits many conservatives in America. In fact, what has reliably distinguished Left from Right in American politics for the past fifty years is a sense of priorities and an opinion about government's purpose. To be on the left has meant to give priority to the end of promoting progress—that is, expanding the domain of individual liberty, particularly in regard to privacy and personal autonomy, and developing a more equal, inclusive society. To be on the left has also meant believing that government has the means and the moral obligation to accomplish the task.

In their agreement over ends or goals, or of what progress consists, progressives in America today differ from their counterparts on the

1. Judith Shklar, "The Liberalism of Fear," in Nancy L. Rosenblum, ed., *Liberalism and the Moral Life* (Cambridge, MA: Harvard University Press, 1989), 21.

right. Although conservatives in America—classical, libertarian, and neoconservative—make a priority of conserving goods that they believe are in danger of being lost or debased, they are nevertheless divided over which moral and political goods are most urgently in need of conservation. In contrast, contemporary progressives—whether they lean toward the center or further left, or whether they draw inspiration from the original Progressive Era reformers, the New Deal, the Great Society and the civil rights movement, or the cultural transformations of the 1960s—are principally divided over the means—the kinds of government action and the sorts of supplements or alternatives to government action—for achieving the progressive end around which they unite. Accordingly, this book focuses on the debates within the party of progress about how to promote it. This is in contrast to the book's companion volume, *Varieties of Conservatism in America*, which deals relatively little with party politics.

The contributors to this volume examine the varieties of progressivism in America from different perspectives and with different expertise. Two are journalists, two are professors of political science who specialize in political philosophy (one of whom served as Deputy Assistant for Domestic Policy to President Clinton), one is a law professor, and one is a sociologist and policy analyst. All think and write beyond their professional niches. Some are more descriptive in their chapters; some are more prescriptive. Although all proceed from a progressive point of view, no effort was made to achieve a common voice, impose a uniform terminology, or elaborate a shared view of American politics; instead, the varieties of voice, terminology, and view on display in this volume combine to give a better sense of the varieties of progressivism in America.

Part I deals with Old Democrats. To understand who they are, and the shape they gave to the modern Democratic Party, it is necessary, according to Ruy Teixeira, to return to the party's origins in the New Deal. The party's governing idea was straightforward: government should help the average person by regulating capitalism and shielding the less advantaged from the vicissitudes of the market. Its worldview "had deep roots in an economy dominated by mass-production industries, [and] was politically based among the workers, overwhelmingly white, in those industries." Indeed, the Democratic Party became the party of the white working class and, through their support, the dominant party in America. But much has changed in the past eighty years. As manufacturing jobs in America decreased and the service sector grew, the size and influence of the Democrats' traditional blue collar constituency shrank. Moreover, many working-class members felt estranged by the cultural upheavals of the 1960s, along with the more strident side of the civil rights movement. They associated the attacks on the family and on the traditional virtues of hard work and self-restraint with the student uprisings, feminists, anti-war activists, consumer advocates, and environmentalists. And they believed they were asked to shoulder an unfair portion of the burden—high taxes to support welfare reform and the turbulence of forced integration of their schools—of achieving social justice.

The initial response of the Old Democrats to the changes over the years was to maintain their commitment to New Deal welfare state policies while opening their party to a diversity of left-wing voices and policies. The white working class, however, refused to go along, resulting in George McGovern's massive defeat in 1972, Ronald Reagan's election in 1980, and Reagan's landslide re-election in 1984. In response, the New Democrats arose to reform the party, to persuade it to shed its image as captive to the idea of "big government" and the programs of "tax-and-spend liberalism," and to craft a message more congenial to middle-class interests and values. It fell to Bill Clinton to adapt the New Democrat message to electoral realities. In fact, contends Teixeira, this adaptation involved a synthesis of New Democrat solicitude for the upwardly mobile middle class and Old Democrat devotion to ambitious government programs aimed at the less well-off. Gore's defeat in 2000, in Teixeira's view, was not a consequence of the fragility of the Clinton synthesis but rather a reflection of the candidate's unfortunate limitations. According to Teixeira, neither should one be misled by the war on terror. Although the war has delayed the formation of what he has argued is an emerging progressive majority, the task for progressives, he believes, is clear: they must remain true to their roots by defending the common man and woman against big corporations and the very wealthy while keeping up with the changing composition of their constituency by reaching out to minorities and to the college-educated professionals in America's large urban centers.

Thomas Edsall is largely in agreement with Teixeira about the origins of modern progressive liberalism in the New Deal and its development over the past seventy-five years, but he poses in stark terms the electoral challenge that the progressive coalition in America now faces. It no longer rests on the overwhelmingly male world of organized labor. Instead, Edsall bluntly writes, it consists, on the one hand, of "an alliance of the so-called subdominant, who are joined by the shared goal of seeking a haven from market pressures as well as insulation from majoritarian moral and social norms that are often experienced as discriminatory." On the other hand, it includes the growing legions of highly educated voters, typically working in professions that require advanced degrees and centered in major metropolitan areas. The new Democratic professional class wants a party that reflects its devotion to "a range of recently democratized rights centered on autonomy, self-development, and individualism."

It was its successes, argues Edsall, that account, in large measure, for the progressive coalition's dramatic transformation. The very policies and social reforms their party championed propelled the working class "have-nots," the original mainstay of the coalition, into the comfortable middle class, thus making them "haves." Edsall agrees with Teixeira that as the 1960s and 1970s unfolded, working-class Democrats found themselves increasingly at odds with the party's intensifying focus on race, reproductive rights, criminal defendant rights, welfare rights, and anti–Vietnam War protests, as well as unhappy with the growing tax burden their party supported, in particular for programs that they believed were taking away their jobs. They also saw their schools disrupted by forced integration while upper-middle-class whites who vigorously supported these policies remained untouched by their dislocating effects. The tensions have persisted. Today, the progressive coalition combines "a socially liberal, well-educated, secular Left leadership cohort, aligned with racial minorities . . . and other previously marginalized groups." This mix of progressive constituencies, Edsall suggests, gives rise to two big questions: Can the coalition hold? And can a movement continue to be considered progressive if it increasingly abandons the aim of representing working-class voters?

Part II explores the contribution of New Democrats. William Galston identifies several forces that fueled the movement's rise: interparty competition in the wake of repeated defeats in presidential elections, the transformation of the American economy from industrial to postindustrial, and the introduction of new ideas by members of the party elite. But Galston, who played important roles in the story he tells—as issues director to Walter Mondale in the 1984 campaign; as a founding member of the Democratic Leadership Council, the flagship organization of the New Democrats; and as Deputy Assistant for Domestic Policy to President Clinton—maintains that the formulation of new ideas was the biggest factor in the success of the New Democrats. Indeed, in 1989, along with Elaine Kamarck, Galston coauthored "The Politics of Evasion," a manifesto that laid out general themes—in opposition both to Reagan-style conservatism and to the left-liberalism of its own party—that would come to define the New Democrats' governing agenda. Galston and Kamarck proceeded from observations about the growing importance of personal independence, the increase in middle-class mobility, and the need for market-based solutions to progressive challenges. From there, they argued for equal opportunity, as opposed to both unregulated competition and equal outcomes. They favored reciprocal responsibility between the individual and the state in contrast, on the one hand, to a regime of pure individualism and, on the other, to a regime of lavish entitlements. And they affirmed the importance of community as an alternative to promoting morals through the law and to ignoring morals and attending only to claims about rights.

Out of these observations and themes, the New Democrats developed a variety of policies. They supported fiscal discipline, calling for cuts in government programs and for the closing of corporate tax loopholes. They emphasized education and training. They favored a dramatic expansion of the Earned Income Tax Credit. They sought to align social programs with middle-class values through market-based health care reform, welfare reform, increases to the size of police forces, and a program of voluntary national service. They called for a shift in foreign policy, arguing that American diplomacy and America's armed forces should serve not only our conventional national security interests but also our democratic ideals. Galston credits President Clinton with several successes in translating New Democrat policy into practice: deficit reduction; free trade promotion (by presiding over passage of NAFTA and a round of GATT negotiations); and, over the strenuous objections of many in his party, welfare reform in 1996. Galston also blames the president and his scandal-ridden second term for squandering a golden opportunity to consolidate New Democrat gains. Although they remain a major source of progressive ideas in the post-Clinton era, the New Democrats continue to fail, Galston observes with regret, to achieve grassroots support for their visions of progress.

Franklin Foer begins his analysis with the heady sense of triumphalism that the New Democrats displayed in the summer of 2000 at the national convention that nominated Al Gore and Joe Lieberman. In the wake of Howard Dean's ascent in the 2003 primary campaign and Lieberman's failure to gain traction, much less inspire enthusiasm, that heady moment seems ancient history. What explains the rapid descent into malaise? As Edsall contended in regard to the

Old Democrats, so Foer maintains about New Democrats—their success brought about their downfall. Having effectively pushed their party, under Clinton's leadership, to embrace middle-class values, pursue fiscal restraint, and recognize the value of community, religion, and patriotism, they left themselves, after Gore's defeat, without a coherent purpose and their party without an urgent need for them.

To be sure, maintains Foer, progressives are united in many policy areas. In economics, all wings of the party recognize the importance of fiscal restraint. On affirmative action, the New Democrat critics and the Old Democrat proponents have largely accepted the status quo. And on the question of old-fashioned Democratic populism, the New Democrats in campaign 2004, according to Foer, have moved a few steps to the left, criticizing corporations, free trade, and the Bush administration for policies they believe tilt decidedly toward the wealthy and the extremely wealthy. In the wake of the war on terror, however, a genuine divide has emerged on the question of foreign policy. Foer worries that, just as the dovish, multilateralist side of the party has found its voice, the New Democrats have fallen silent about the need for a vigorous defense abroad of both America's interests and ideals. However, in harmony with Galston he believes that the most important challenge for the New Democrats is to move beyond the world of Washington think tanks and Georgetown dinner parties, where they are most comfortable, and develop a broader constituency for a program of progressive reform built on middle-class values and the realities of the postindustrial economy.

Part III assesses the future of progressivism in America. David Cole asks what a progressive lawyer can do when progressives do not control any of the three branches of government. Progressives are still adjusting. The heyday of progressive lawyers ran from about 1953 to 1986, from the Warren court through the Burger court. For more than three decades, the Supreme Court acted as a significant force for social change, handing down such landmark decisions as *Brown v. Board of Education* (1954, declaring segregation in public schools illegal), *Gideon v. Wainright* (1963, extending the right to a lawyer, paid for by the state, to all indigent persons under interrogation or indictment in the criminal system), *Miranda v. Arizona* (1966, requiring that police inform accused of their rights), *Roe v. Wade* (1973, holding that the constitution protects a woman's right to terminate her pregnancy), *Craig v. Boren* (1976, declaring sex discrimination presumptively invalid), and *Bakke v. Regents of California* (1978, upholding the constitutionality of using race as a factor in university admissions). The election of Ronald Reagan, argues Cole, changed all that. Reagan made a political issue of federal judicial appointments, attacking judicial activism and placing hundreds of conservatives on the bench. The first President Bush continued the work. Today, progressives face not only a judiciary that is less sympathetic to the use of the courts for progressive reform but also, as a result of progressive achievements over the past fifty years, a range of more systemic and less soluble problems.

In response, maintains Cole, progressives have shifted substantive commitments and tactics. First, they have largely abandoned the ambitious demand that courts recognize "affirmative rights"—that is, enforceable obligations on the part of government to provide social and economic benefits so that citizens can effectively exercise their basic rights. Instead, progressives have stressed the more limited claim that courts should ensure that rights enjoyed by some should be enjoyed equally by all. Second, they have adopted utilitarian arguments in favor of rights they believe are essential for respecting human dignity. So, they argue, the right to a decent level of material goods and the right to education should also be supported because they benefit society as a whole. Third, they have begun to look beyond federal courts by taking their arguments for progressive reform to the political branches of government, to state courts, or directly to the people. In keeping with this refocus, they have come to see lawsuits that they do bring in federal courts not as self-contained interventions but as one front in a concerted effort to educate and mobilize the public. Fourth, they have looked outward to international law, universal human rights, and other nations' constitutions as the basis for legal arguments to effect change in U.S. courts. In sum, Cole believes that progressive lawyers in America have advanced their cause by refining their understanding of the factors affecting, and the trade-offs inherent, in progressive reform.

Jeffrey Isaac concludes the volume with a reassessment of the overall prospects of progressivism in America. Like Cole, Isaac presents a chastened prognosis. Contrary to the hopes for a progressive revival that were developed by a number of influential authors in the mid-1990s, as well as to those hopes that received expression in books published after George W. Bush became president, which argued that his election was an anomaly and that demographic, cultural, and economic trends point toward a new progressive hegemony, Isaac sees a political climate that is inhospitable to dramatic progressive change. It's not that Isaac believes that conservatism in America is on the ascendance. Rather, Isaac argues that features of contemporary America that he calls postmodern are thwarting the consolidation of a progressive coalition. Among the most notable of these features are a "'post-Fordist' economy characterized by extreme forms of flexibility and mobility that defy regulatory mechanisms and that severely test the capacities of the nation-state; new forms of consumerism and consumer credit that severely weaken the 'organic solidarities' that in the past grounded oppositional social and political movements; and especially new forms of communication . . . that profoundly call into question the progressive assumption of any kind of rational public or meaningful public discourse about public problems and their solution." The result is that American society has become inhospitable to large-scale political movements, however much progressives may believe that the claims of equality demand them.

What is the best progressive response? Isaac examines a variety of writings that, over the past decade or so, have emphasized the role that civil society and its voluntary organizations can play in the advancement of generally progressive ends. He is largely in agreement with proponents of "the new citizenship" and "the third way" that "an ambitious agenda of political reform and socioeconomic regulation is unlikely to be enacted; thus, more modest and localized efforts represent the best hope for a left-liberal politics of democratic problem solving and public regulation." Yet even as he affirms that this chastened approach has much to recommend itself under current circumstances, he insists that progressives must acknowledge its disadvantages from a progressive point of view. Indeed, he goes so far as to characterize the gap that has opened between the pursuit of progressive ends and the viability of mobilizing majorities on their behalf as the "tragedy" of progressive liberalism. But he still insists on the moral and political imperative to search out opportunities to promote progress through the pragmatic, piecemeal initiatives now available.

The debate among progressives about the most suitable means for the promotion of progressive ends persists. The choice depends on shifting coalitions; political leadership; developments in culture, economics, demography, and technology; and unforeseeable actions and events beyond our borders. It is unlikely, though, that progressives can afford to confine themselves to contending with this complex of factors. There is no reason to suppose either that progress has no costs or that progress does not depend on dimensions of moral and political life to which conservatives give particular attention and for which they acquire special expertise. It may well be that progressives need conservatives—just as conservatives need progressives—not only to keep them honest and energetic, but also to keep them apprized of those human goods that they have less practice in recognizing and honoring. Certainly such a lesson is taught by that larger liberalism that orients, spurs, and restrains the varieties of progressivism, as well as the varieties of conservatism, in America.

PART ONE

Old Democrats

CHAPTER ONE

Old Democrats and the Shock of the New

Ruy Teixeira

WHO ARE THE Old Democrats? A better question is: Who *were* the Old Democrats? If we are to understand those labeled Old Democrats today (Ted Kennedy, Dick Gephardt) and the role they and their ideas have played in the evolution of the Democratic Party, we need to go back several decades to the era when Old Democrats worthy of the name still roamed the earth.

Old Democrats

Old Democrats were New Deal Democrats. Their worldview was based on a combination of the Democratic Party's historic populist commitment to the average working American and their own experience in battling the Great Depression (and building their political coalition) through increased government spending and the regulation and promotion of labor unions. It was really a rather simple philosophy, even if its application was complex: Government should help the average person through government spending. Capitalism needs regulation to work properly. Labor unions are good. Putting money in the average person's pocket is more important than rarified worries about the quality of life. Traditional morality is to be respected not challenged. Racism and the like are bad, but not so bad that the party should depart from its main mission of material uplift for the average American.

The Old Democrat worldview, which had deep roots in an economy dominated by mass-production industries, was politically based among the workers, who were overwhelmingly white. Their dominance among these voters was, in turn, the key to their political success. To be sure, there were important divisions among these voters—by country of origin (German, Scandinavian, Eastern European, English, Irish, Italian, etc.), by religion (Protestants vs. Catholics), and by region (South vs. non-South)—that greatly complicated the politics of this group, but the Old Democrats mastered these complications and maintained a deep base among these voters.

Of course, the New Deal Coalition, as originally forged, included most blacks and was certainly cross-class, especially among groups like Jews and Southerners. But the prototypical member of the coalition was an ethnic white worker—commonly seen as those working in a unionized factory but also including those who weren't in unions or who toiled in other blue-collar settings (construction, transportation, etc.). It was these voters who provided the numbers for four Franklin Roosevelt election victories, as well as Harry Truman's narrow victory in 1948,[1] and who provided political support for the emerging U.S. welfare state, with its implicit social contract and greatly expanded role for government.

Even in the 1950s, with Republican Dwight Eisenhower as president, the white working class continued to put Democrats in Congress and to support the expansion of the welfare state, as a roaring U.S. economy delivered the goods and government poured money

1. Ruy Teixeira and Joel Rogers, *America's Forgotten Majority: Why the White Working Class Still Matters* (New York: Basic Books, 2000), 5.

into roads, science, schools, and whatever else seemed necessary to build up the country. This era, stretching back to the late 1940s and forward to the mid-1960s, was the era that created the first mass middle class in the world—a middle class that even factory workers could enter because they could earn relatively comfortable livings without high levels of education or professional skills. A middle class, in other words, that members of the white working class could reasonably aspire to and frequently attain.

So, Old Democrats depended on the white working class for political support and the white working class depended on the Democrats to run government and the economy in a way that kept the upward escalator to the middle class moving. Social and cultural issues were not particularly important to this mutually beneficial relationship; indeed, these issues had only a peripheral role in the uncomplicated progressivism that animated the Democratic Party of the 1930s, 1940s, and 1950s. But that arrangement, and that uncomplicated progressivism, could not survive the decline of mass-production industries and the rise of postindustrial capitalism.

First, there was the transformation of the white working class itself. In 1948, about two-thirds of the workforce was white men, and the bulk of these white men worked at blue-collar manufacturing and construction jobs or at blue-collar service jobs, such as janitor or warehouseman. These men were also heavily unionized, especially in certain areas of the country: by the late 1940s, unions claimed around 60 percent or more of the Northern blue-collar workforce.[2] But the past half century has changed all that. The white working class has become much more diverse—today, there are almost as many women workers as men—even as unionization has declined. Only a relatively small proportion (17 percent) of the white working class works in

2. All data in this paragraph come from John B. Judis and Ruy Teixeira, *The Emerging Democratic Majority* (New York: Scribner, 2002), 62–65.

manufacturing (even among men, the proportion is still less than 25 percent). In fact, the entire goods-producing sector, which includes construction, mining, and agriculture, as well as manufacturing, only covers 30 percent of the white working class. This leaves the over-whelming majority—seven in ten—in the service sector, including government. There are almost as many members of the new white working class in trade alone (especially retail) as there are in all goods-producing jobs.[3]

Second, as this great transformation was changing the character of the white working class, reducing the size and influence of the Democrats' traditional blue-collar constituencies, the evolution of postindustrial capitalism was creating new constituencies and move-ments with new demands. These new constituencies and movements wanted more out of the welfare state than steady economic growth, copious infrastructure spending, and the opportunity to raise a family in the traditional manner.

During the 1960s, these new demands on the welfare state came to a head. Americans' concern about their quality of life overflowed from the two-car garage to clean air and water and safe automobiles, from higher wages to government-guaranteed health care in old age, and from job access to equal opportunities for men and women and blacks and whites. Out of these concerns came the environmental, consumer, civil rights, and feminist movements. As Americans aban-doned the older ideal of self-denial and the taboos that accompanied it, they embraced a libertarian ethic of personal life. Women asserted their sexual independence through the use of birth control pills and through exercising the right to have an abortion. Adolescents exper-imented with sex and courtship. Homosexuals "came out" and openly congregated in bars and neighborhoods.

Of these changes, the one with the most far-reaching political

3. All data in this paragraph came from Teixeira and Rogers, *America's Forgotten Majority*, 17.

effects was the civil rights movement and its demands for equality and economic progress for black America. Democrats, because of both their traditional, if usually downplayed, antiracist ideology and their political relationship to the black community, had no choice but to respond to those demands. The result was a great victory for social justice, but one that created huge political difficulties for the Democrats among their white working-class supporters. Kevin Phillips captured these developments:

> The principal force which broke up the Democratic (New Deal) coalition is the Negro socioeconomic revolution and liberal Democratic ideological inability to cope with it. Democratic "Great Society" programs aligned that party with many Negro demands, but the party was unable to defuse the racial tension sundering the nation. The South, the West, and the Catholic sidewalks of New York were the focus points of conservative opposition to the welfare liberalism of the federal government; however, the general opposition . . . came in large part from prospering Democrats who objected to Washington dissipating their tax dollars on programs which did them no good. The Democratic party fell victim to the ideological impetus of a liberalism which had carried it beyond programs taxing the few for the benefit of the many . . . to programs taxing the many on behalf of the few.[4]

However, if race was the chief vehicle by which the New Deal coalition was torn apart, it was by no means the only one. White working-class voters also reacted poorly to the extremes with which the rest of the new social movements became identified. Feminism became identified with bra-burners, lesbians, and hostility to the nuclear family; the antiwar movement, with appeasement of the Third World radicals and the Soviet Union; the environmental movement, with a Luddite opposition to economic growth; and the move toward

---

4. Kevin Phillips, *The Emerging Republican Majority* (New York: Arlington House, 1969).

more personal freedom, with a complete abdication of personal responsibility.

Thus, the Old Democrat mainstream that dominated the party was confronted with a challenge. The uncomplicated New Deal commitments to government spending, economic regulation, and labor unions that had defined Democratic progressivism for more than thirty years suddenly provided little guidance for dealing with an explosion of potential new constituencies for the party. The demands of the new constituencies for equality and for a better, as opposed to merely a richer, life were starting to redefine what progressivism meant, and the Democrats had to struggle to catch up.

New Old Democrats

Initially, Old Democrat politicians responded to these changes in the fashion of politicians since time immemorial: they sought to co-opt these new movements by absorbing many of their demands while holding onto the party's basic ideology and style of governing. Thus were born the *New* Old Democrats.

New Old Democrats didn't change their fundamental commitment to the New Deal welfare state; instead, they grafted onto it support for all the various new constituencies and their key demands. After Lyndon Johnson signed the Civil Rights Act in 1964, the party moved, during the next eight years, to give the women's, antiwar, consumers', and environmental movements prominent places within the party. This move reflected both the politician's standard interest in capturing the votes of new constituencies *and* the ongoing expansion of the definition of what it meant to be a Democrat, particularly a progressive one.

There was no guarantee, of course, that gains among these new constituencies wouldn't be more than counterbalanced by losses among their old constituency—the white working class—who had precious little interest in this expansion of what it meant to be a progressive and a Democrat. Indeed, in 1972, that turned out to be the case with the nomination and disastrous defeat of George McGovern—an enthusiastic New Old Democrat. McGovern's commitment to the traditional Democratic welfare state was unmistakable, but so was his commitment to all the various social movements and constituencies that were reshaping the party, the demands of which were enshrined in his campaign platform. That made it easy for Richard Nixon's campaign to typecast McGovern as the candidate of "acid, amnesty, and abortion." The white working class reacted accordingly and gave Nixon overwhelming support at the polls, casting 70 percent of their votes for the Republican candidate.[5]

Indeed, just how far the Democratic Party fell in the eyes of the white working class during that time can be seen by comparing the average white working-class vote for the Democrats in 1960–1964 (55 percent) with their average vote for the Democrats in 1968–1972 (35 percent).[6] That's a drop of 20 points, from over half to just over one-third. The Democrats were the party of the white working class no longer.

With the sharp economic recession and Nixon scandals of 1973–1974, the Democrats were able to develop enough political momentum to retake the White House in 1976, with Jimmy Carter's narrow defeat of Gerald Ford. But their political revival did not last long. Not only did the Carter administration fail to do much to defuse white working class hostility to the new social movements, especially to the black liberation movement, but also economic events—the stagflation of the late 1970s—conspired to make that hostility even sharper. Though stagflation (inflation and unemployment combined with slow economic growth) first appeared during the 1973–1975 recession, it persisted during the Carter administration and was peaking on the eve of the 1980 election. As the economy slid once more

5. Teixeira and Rogers, *America's Forgotten Majority*, 6.
6. Ibid., 32.

into recession, the inflation rate in that year was 12.5 percent. Combined with an unemployment rate of 7.1 percent, it produced a "misery index" of nearly 20 percent.

The stagflation fed resentments about race—about high taxes for welfare (which were assumed to go primarily to minorities) and about affirmative action. It also sowed doubts about Democrats' ability to manage the economy and made Republican and business explanations of stagflation—blaming it on government regulation, high taxes, and spending—more plausible. In 1978, the white backlash and doubts about Democratic economic policies helped fuel a nationwide tax revolt. In 1980, these factors reproduced the massive exodus of white working-class voters from the Democratic tickets first seen in 1968 and 1972. In the 1980 and 1984 elections, Reagan averaged 61 percent support among the white working class, compared with an average of 35 percent support for his Democratic opponents, Jimmy Carter and Walter Mondale.[7]

New Democrats

New Old Democrats appeared powerless to stop this juggernaut, saddled as they were with a double-barreled progressivism that increasingly seemed like a dual liability. On the one hand, they were committed to a model of the welfare state economy that no longer worked, and on the other, they were tied to a set of constituency groups whose priorities seemed alien to middle America. When their preferred candidate, Walter Mondale, got blown away in the 1984 election, losing every state but Minnesota and the District of Columbia, some Democrats decided enough was enough and organized a group to shed these electoral liabilities and reform the party.

The group was the Democratic Leadership Council (DLC), founded in 1985, and it directly counterposed its "New Democrat"

7. Ibid.

approach to that of Mondale and the New Old Democrats who dominated the party. In a memo to prospective DLC members, Al
Fromm, cofounder of the group along with Will Marshall, expressed
his concern about the Democrats' decline, which he blamed on the
"consistent pursuit of wrongheaded, losing strategies." Fromm was
particularly critical of Mondale's strategy of "making blatant appeals
to liberal and minority interest groups in the hopes of building a
winning coalition where a majority, under normal circumstances, simply does not exist." Fromm also worried that with union membership
declining, the Democrats "are more and more viewed as the party of
'big labor,'" and that with liberalism in disrepute, Democrats are
"increasingly viewed as the 'liberal' party." Fromm was most at home
with Southern Democrats like Sam Nunn, Chuck Robb, and Russell
Long. Although he supported social security and other basic New
Deal reforms, was concerned about poverty, and was committed to
civil rights, he parted company with New Old Democrats by being
strongly sympathetic to business's view of its own problems, hostile
or indifferent to labor unions, and opposed to any ambitious new
government social programs.[8]

After Michael Dukakis's defeat in 1988, Fromm, Marshall, and
the DLC decided to develop a philosophy and a platform for the
Democratic Party that would redefine what it meant to be a progressive. With money raised primarily by Wall Street Democrats, the
DLC set up the Progressive Policy Institute (PPI), with Marshall at
the helm, and hired policy experts to draft papers and proposals. The
most important of these was a 1989 paper entitled "The Politics of
Evasion," written by William Galston, Mondale's former issues director, and PPI fellow Elaine Kamarck, who would later become Gore's
policy adviser in the first Clinton administration. Galston and
Kamarck argued that in the late 1960s, the liberalism of the New
Deal had degenerated into a "liberal fundamentalism," which

---

8. Judis and Teixeira, *The Emerging Democratic Majority*, 127.

the public has come to associate with tax and spending policies that contradict the interests of average families; with welfare policies that foster dependence rather than self-reliance; with softness toward the perpetrators of crime and indifference toward its victims; with ambivalence toward the assertion of American values and interests abroad; and with an adversarial stance toward mainstream moral and cultural values.[9]

Galston, Kamarck, and the DLC advocated fiscal conservatism, welfare reform, increased spending on crime through the development of a police corps, tougher mandatory sentences, support for capital punishment, and policies that encouraged traditional families. Another PPI fellow, David Osborne, developed a strategy for "reinventing government" by contracting out services while retaining control over how they were performed. In Osborne's formulation, government should "steer, not row."

As can readily be seen, the DLC New Democrats were challenging the double-barreled progressivism of the New Old Democrats across the board, from their backing of new constituency groups and those groups' policy positions to their attachment to New Deal–style social spending and regulation. They were also arguing that only their strategy could be effective in winning back the white working class—the New Old Democrats' original constituency.

Beyond their claims about reaching the white working class, the DLC and PPI strategists didn't really detail the constituencies they were trying to reach. One can infer from their writings that they were targeting middle-class, white-collar suburbanites, but there was little specific guidance beyond that as to where Democrats should seek votes among this very broad group. They also didn't talk about how a majority would appear on a map; instead, their focus seemed to be primarily on winning the Midwest and the South for Democrats. The DLC was skeptical about California being the anchor of a new major-

9. William Galston and Elaine Kamarck, "The Politics of Evasion: Democrats and the Presidency," Progressive Policy Institute, September 1989.

ity—Galston and Kamarck derided this idea as "the California dream." The DLC also didn't put stock in the power of the women's vote to deliver a new majority: Galston and Kamarck wrote that "the gender gap that has opened up in the past twelve years is not the product of a surge of Democratic support among women, but rather the erosion of Democratic support among men." The DLC's 1990 platform didn't even explicitly support abortion rights.

In other words, the DLC understood neither the special role that professionals, women, and minorities would play in the new Democratic majority nor the central role that California and the Northwest would play. The role of these groups only became clear in the next decade, as Bill Clinton adapted the New Democrat formula to electoral realities and, in the process, created a synthesis between the politics of the New Democrats and the politics of the New Old Democrats who still dominated large sectors of the party.

The Clinton Synthesis

It is simplistic to think of Bill Clinton as purely a New Democrat. The reality is considerably more complicated. Indeed, although his debt to the New Democrats and the DLC is large and obvious, he is also responsible for taking the views of the New Old Democrats— both the New (social movements) and the Old (New Deal)—and making them part of an electorally effective politics. In other words, while his success in the 1990s marked the ascendance of New Democrat politics, it also consolidated the influence on the party of the new social movements *and* preserved the influence of moderate New Deal populism and activism on the party's program. It helped turn what had been shaping up as a war between two different versions of progressivism into a synthesis that all elements of the party could accept, however grudgingly.

Consider how Clinton ran his first successful campaign for president. It is true that he espoused a number of New Democrat themes from the very beginning of his campaign. To inoculate himself against Republican attacks, he championed welfare reform, spending on police and public safety, and capital punishment. He spoke of a "new covenant" between the people and the government—"a solemn agreement between the people and their government, based not simply on what each of us can take, but what all of us must give to our nation." But as the heir of a Southern-Southwestern populism, which had included Democratic politicians like Lyndon Johnson, Albert Gore Sr., Dale Bumpers, and Oklahoman Fred Harris, and as a product of the antiestablishment student movements of the 1960s, Clinton did not hesitate to emphasize his populist streak when it became necessary to defeat neoliberal Paul Tsongas, whose views on economics paralleled those of the DLC. Like Mondale against Hart in 1984, Clinton ran as a champion of the New Deal. He charged Tsongas with a lack of faith in Social Security; he promised a large middle-class tax cut, massive public investments, and national health insurance. He avidly courted unions, blacks, and senior citizens. And, in the end, he prevailed against Tsongas.

In the general election campaign, he tacked back to the center. He still trumpeted his support for women's rights and for the environment, and with the country mired in recession, he continued to promise ambitious new programs, as epitomized by his populist-style platform statement, "Putting People First." But Clinton also emphasized his support for reducing government bureaucracy and for "ending welfare as we know it." In the end, Clinton's campaign—and his election victory—reflected a synthesis of New Democrat and New Old Democrat themes, not simply an application of the DLC's strategic insights, as that organization's mythology presents it.

This synthesis was also on full display in Clinton's successful 1996 campaign. Clinton, the populist reinforced by an AFL-CIO that had been reinvigorated politically under its new president John Sweeney, flayed the Republicans for cutting Medicare to pay for a tax cut to the wealthy. Clinton, the former DLC chairman, boasted of reforming welfare and advanced incremental, not "big government," reforms to make higher education affordable, put computers in classrooms, and provide child care and increased access to health care. Clinton, a child of the 1960s, campaigned earnestly for civil rights, women's rights, and the protection of the environment. And Clinton, the tribune of postindustrial America, promised to "build a bridge to the twenty-first century."

The election results showed the electoral promise of Clinton's new synthesis. He carried women by 16 points (including white women by 5 points), professionals by 17 points, and even white working-class voters by 1 point.[10] He totally dominated the minority vote, receiving 76 percent support, and easily carried the new Democratic bastion of California (by 13 points), as well as the rest of the Pacific Northwest. He also carried key Midwestern swing states, such as Ohio and Missouri; much of the Southwest (New Mexico, Arizona, and Nevada); and four Southern states, including Florida.

The latter part of Clinton's second term, of course, was heavily colored by the Monica Lewinsky sex scandal and Clinton's subsequent impeachment. And unfortunately for the Democrats, with that scandal and its cultural implications as a background, Al Gore was hardly the ideal candidate to rise to the challenge of making the Clinton synthesis work in the 2000 election.

But this wasn't because the synthesis was alien to Gore's background and viewpoint. He was certainly a New Democrat. He had been a founding member of the DLC and the choice of some of its leaders for president in 1988.

In addition, as a student at Harvard, Gore had become familiar with, and participated in, the social movements of the 1960s, particularly the environmental movement, for which he later wrote a book, *Earth in the Balance*. He had also inherited his father's populist con-

10. Author's analysis of 1996 National Election Study and 1996 Voter News Service Exit Poll data.

victions. So, like Clinton, Gore had different sides and faces, but in public he could exhibit them only over time and, in contrast to Clinton, in a manner that made his audience question whether they were seeing the real Al Gore or a campaign contrivance. This turned out to hurt in an election where the problems of trust and being perceived as culturally elitist loomed large due to the Clinton scandals.

Consistent with his tin ear for the synthesis, Gore lurched every few months of his presidential campaign from one face and strategy to another. First, under the tutelage of Mark Penn, the DLC's pollster, Gore tried aiming his message at "wired workers" (workers who "frequently use computers that are part of a network and work together in teams"), who were allegedly concerned about the threat of "suburban sprawl" to a better "quality of life." That strategy didn't work (in October 1999, Gore trailed Bush by 19 percent in one opinion poll and had lost his lead to his Democratic challenger, former Senator Bill Bradley, in Iowa and New Hampshire), so he fired Penn and brought on a group of more conventionally liberal consultants.

Gore next adopted the same strategy against Bradley that Mondale had used against Hart and that Clinton had used against Tsongas. He defended Democratic orthodoxy and the party's most loyal constituencies. With the resulting solid support from union members and blacks, he easily defeated Bradley for the nomination. But having vanquished Bradley, Gore found himself once more trailing Bush. So, like Mondale and Clinton before him, Gore's initial reaction was to grasp for the center, emphasizing issues like fiscal responsibility. This time, however, the trick didn't work. A month passed, and Gore was still consistently trailing Bush, with a double-digit deficit in many opinion polls.

So Gore brought in yet another consultant, Stanley Greenberg, Clinton's pollster in 1992. Greenberg advised Gore to use his biography, particularly his service in Vietnam, to counteract voters' identification of him with the Clinton scandals, to steer clear of Clinton himself, and to underplay his support for issues like gun control and abortion that could alienate working-class voters. Greenberg also recommended that Gore resume the populist rhetoric of the primary campaign, but without committing himself to any large government programs. Gore's convention speech did exactly this. He said of the Republicans, "They're for the powerful, and we're for the people." After the convention speech, Gore suddenly sped past Bush in the opinion polls and remained ahead for a month until the fateful debates, when his personal limitations as a candidate shone through. In the end, of course, he lost, albeit by a very, very narrow (and contested) electoral vote margin (271–267).

As this recounting suggests, Gore was a poor bearer indeed of the Clinton synthesis and never could figure out a way to make that synthesis come alive for voters. Instead, he tended to harp on one aspect or another of the synthesis to the exclusion of others. Voters found these shifting personae unattractive, and that image dovetailed all too well with a cultural distrust of the national Democratic Party that had been exacerbated by the Clinton scandals. All of this was enough to cost Gore an extremely close election.

Newer Democrats

Gore did win the popular vote (48.4 to 47.9 percent), however, and the 267 electoral votes he received represented states that Clinton had also carried twice. All of those states, which included California (by an easy 12-point margin, despite having done little campaigning there), Oregon and Washington in the Pacific Northwest, New Mexico in the Southwest, Illinois and New Jersey (carried by the Republicans in every presidential election between 1968 and 1988), and every New England state but New Hampshire, had now been carried by the Democrats three elections in a row. These states were the Democrats' new base and showed how the geographical strength of the Democratic coalition had shifted.

Gore's performance was also solid among the Democrats' emerging constituencies, indicating the consolidation of the constituencies within the Democratic Party. He received 75 percent of the minority vote (which was about a fifth of the vote in 2000 and will likely be a quarter by the end of the decade) and actually did better than Clinton among both blacks and Asians. He carried professionals by 7 points and women by 11 points. Moreover, he did particularly well among the subcategories of women that are growing the fastest: Single, working women—who have grown from 19 percent of the adult female population in 1970 to 29 percent today—backed Gore 67 to 29 percent. College-educated women—who have grown from just 8 percent of the 25-and-older female population to 24 percent today— backed Gore over Bush by 57 to 39 percent.[11] Gore also carried America's burgeoning postindustrial metropolitan areas, or "ideopolises" (where 44 percent of the nation's voters now live), by 55 to 41 percent. These technologically advanced areas, specializing in the production of ideas and services, are now as central to today's Democratic coalition as the manufacturing centers of the industrial economy were to the New Deal coalition.

Where Gore most severely underperformed relative to Clinton was among white working-class voters. He lost them by 17 points, whereas Clinton had carried them by 1 point in 1996. Gore's deficit included a walloping by 34 points among white working-class men.[12]

The recriminations for Gore's loss flew thick and fast after the election. Predictably, the DLC blamed his defeat on his failure to hew strictly to the New Democrat line. In so doing, they frequently sounded like they were simply replaying the tapes they'd made back in the 1980s when analyzing the Mondale and Dukakis defeats. It was as if the Democratic Party of 2001—after all the changes of the Clinton era—had somehow become the Democratic Party of 1989

11. All election data in this paragraph from author's analysis of 2000 National Election Study and 2000 Voter News Service Exit Poll data.

12. Author's analysis of 2000 Voter News Service Exit Poll data.

or even 1985, and the very same battles had to be reenacted, Ground-hog Day–style.

"Gore chose a populist rather than a New Democrat message," DLC leader Al Fromm wrote. "As a result, voters viewed him as too liberal and identified him as an advocate of big government. Those perceptions . . . hurt him with male voters in general and with key New Economy swing voters in particular. By emphasizing class warfare, he seemed to be talking to Industrial Age America, not Information Age America." The legacy of the Clinton scandals or Gore's particular failings as a candidate were nowhere to be found in this explanation.

It's important to note that the liberal, or New Old Democrat, wing of the party did not take the mirror image stance of the New Democrats, which would have been to claim Gore lost because he wasn't liberal enough. Instead, they generally backed the analysis of Gore's pollster, Greenberg, who did an extensive postelection poll under the auspices of the liberal Campaign for America's Future. Greenberg blamed Gore's defeat primarily on the decline of the Democratic vote among white working-class voters (which was more consistent with data from the exit polls), particularly white working-class men. According to Greenberg, these voters backed Bush rather than Gore because they didn't trust Gore—a sentiment traceable to the Clinton scandals—and because they rejected Gore's stands in favor of gun control and abortion. They were not put off by Gore's populism. On the contrary, it was a major reason that many of them backed him, despite their cultural distaste for Gore himself.[13]

Neither Greenberg nor party liberals, however, had much of an answer for how to advance the synthesis pioneered by Clinton in a closely divided country where conservative Republicans now held the levers of power. It was true that Democrats would be silly to abandon populism, just as it was true that cultural distrust among the white

13. See Judis and Teixeira, *The Emerging Democratic Majority*, 141–43.

working class was a real problem. But the DLC, in their ham-handed way, were right about where the party's future lay. It may not lie in their hobbyhorse of "wired workers," which is much too vague a designation, but it does lie in the new workforce of postindustrial America and in the fast-growing metropolitan areas where they live and work. This workforce responds not to the old-time religion of party liberals but rather to the new progressivism encapsulated by the Clinton synthesis. The key for Democrats, therefore, is to discover a strategy that makes this new progressivism palatable to a sufficient base of white working-class voters while building the support the party needs among college-educated professionals and others in America's burgeoning ideopolises. This latter aspect of the Democrats' task seemed to elude Greenberg and the New Old Democrats.

Given these huge explanatory gaps on both sides, most Democrats were understandably tepid about signing up on either side of the dispute. Both sides seemed more interested in rehearsing old debates and defending old positions than in grappling with the election that had just happened and building on the Clinton synthesis in all its complicated glory. There was simply no appetite among most Democrats for rerunning the faction disputes of the 1980s; Democrats knew their party had changed dramatically in the 1990s, and an argument that was detached from that reality seemed uninteresting at best and downright destructive at worst. Moreover, the Republican Party under Bush, with an ascendant hard Right and its willingness to say or do anything to win, seemed a formidable enemy that called for a fresh Democratic approach, not just old wine in new bottles. This has lead to the emergence of what I call "Newer Democrats."

In the aftermath of the 2000 election, Newer Democrats saw the New Democrats and the New Old Democrats, the DLC and the liberals/populists, as continuing to provide important insights and useful tools for building the party. And both groups were clearly important parts of the party that were not going to go away. But neither New Democrats nor populists, in this emerging view, seemed to know how to beat Bush and the no-holds-barred conservative Right that was taking over the Republican Party. Both groups seemed stuck in the past, even though the urgent task was to transform the actually existing Democratic Party, with its updated vision of progressivism and new coalition, into an instrument that could beat the Bush Republicans.

This new view was accentuated by the events of 2001–2004. Bush started his presidency acting like he'd won a landslide in a country that was thirsting for a radical antigovernment agenda. That willful misinterpretation of the public mood was turbocharged by September 11 and its aftermath, when Bush benefited from the largest and longest "rally effect" the U.S. presidency has ever seen. In effect, Bush took it as a license to ignore public opinion and pursue the agenda nearest and dearest to his heart, the hard-Right agenda of the base of the Republican Party: big tax cuts; containment or outright reduction of nondefense spending; heavily probusiness social and regulatory policy; dismantling of environmental protections; partial privatization of Social Security; appointment of conservative judges; banning the use of federal funds that involved the destruction of embryos for stemcell research; and (after 9/11) an aggressive and, when necessary, go-it-alone foreign policy.

What did Democratic leaders do in response? That is where Newer Democrats found much to question in the conduct of both factions of the party. First, there was the massive tax cut of 2001, which Democrats of all stripes seemed powerless to stop, or even oppose, in a disciplined way. Then, of course, came September 11, when the oddly craven behavior of the Democrats became completely supine. Given the intensity of the rally effect for the president, a conciliatory approach by Democratic politicians was only to be expected. But in the view of many Democrats, that conciliatory approach went too far, especially because concessions on the Democratic side seemed never to be matched with concessions on the Republican side. For example, there was the early 2002 No Child

Left Behind education reform bill, which liberal Democrats like Ted
Kennedy helped pass but then were stiffed on the bill's funding levels.
Then there was the summer of corporate scandals in 2002, when
congressional Democrats let Bush and the GOP off the hook with
the easy-to-sign-onto Sarbanes-Oxley bill, effectively blunting the partisan edge of that issue. It seemed like the Democrats in Congress
were getting rolled, again and again.

But what came after the summer of 2002 really fueled the ascendance of Newer Democrats. That summer saw a shift toward the
Democrats in the polls, both nationally and in key state races. Not
coincidentally, in the eyes of many Democrats, the Bush administration chose the end of the summer to launch a national debate on
whether to go to war with Iraq. The Bush administration had decided
earlier to attempt to oust Iraqi dictator Saddam Hussein, but the
White House staged the congressional debate over the war during the
height of the election rather than before or after it. Rather than
remove the issue of war from political partisanship—as Bush's father
had done in 1990 when he postponed the congressional debate on
whether to forcefully oust Iraq from Kuwait until after the election—
the second Bush White House sought to use the issue for political
ends.

This tactic infuriated many Democrats, but the response of their
own party infuriated them even more. The Democrats in Congress,
guided by Senate Majority Leader Tom Daschle, House Minority
Leader Dick Gephardt, and Terry McAuliffe, the chairman of the
Democratic National Committee, adopted a deeply flawed strategy to
counter the Republicans. They chose to focus on prescription drugs
and social security. These were important issues, but neither was the
central domestic issue to voters. The central issue was the economy,
but, incredibly, Democrats did not offer any economic program to
combat the country's growing unemployment.

As for the Iraq war debate, many of the Democrats, led by
Gephardt, adopted a strategy of simply accepting the administration's

case for war, with all its attendant omissions and exaggerations, in the hope of getting the vote over quickly so that voters would focus on the domestic issues on which the Democrats had an advantage. In early October, Gephardt cut short an attempt at a bipartisan counterresolution on the war by agreeing to an administration proposal. Daschle, and other Democratic leaders, fearing that they would suffer isolation and defeat if they opposed the war resolution, dropped their efforts at forcing a compromise and supported the Bush proposal. Four days after the vote on Iraq, Gephardt gave a major speech heralding the Democrats' social and economic programs but omitting any discussion of the prospect of war with Iraq. Gephardt's ill-conceived strategy allowed Bush free reign. During the last two weeks of the campaign, when Bush launched a whirlwind national tour in support of Republican candidates, rallying the country against the threat to its national security.

Linked with Bush's aggressive campaigning were some dirty campaign tactics in which Democratic candidates' patriotism and commitment to the war on terror were directly and repeatedly impugned. For example, in the Georgia Senate race, Republican Saxby Chambliss, who had never served in the military, attacked incumbent Max Cleland, a war hero who had lost his legs and an arm in Vietnam, for not supporting the Republican plan for the homeland security department. The Republicans even went so far as to run an ad linking Cleland to images of Saddam Hussein and Osama bin Laden.

In the short run at least, Bush's tactics worked. The Republicans had an outstanding election, gaining control of the Senate (and thereby unified control of government) with a two-seat pickup. Their margin in the House increased to 229 seats, to the Democrats' 205, with one Democrat voting independent. This was not the expected result in a first-term, off-year election with a bad economy.

The election results shocked rank-and-file Democrats. And once they got over their shock—helped by Mary Landrieu's run-off December victory in the Louisiana Senate contest—they were furious.

Why were the Republicans getting away with wrapping themselves in the flag while they conducted themselves in a hyperpartisan fashion? Why was the Democratic leadership being so deferential when their only reward was to get stabbed in the back by a Republican leadership and administration that weren't exactly playing by the Marquis of Queensbury rules? Old Democrats like Gephardt—deeply implicated as they were in the Democrats' nonconfrontational and unsuccessful strategy—didn't have any convincing answers. Nor did the DLC and orthodox New Democrat politicians like Joe Lieberman, who had offered some criticisms of the Gephardt-Daschle leadership but who had actually backed Bush's push toward war in Iraq. To increasing numbers of Democrats, it seemed like both factions of the party had had their chances—and had blown it.

That judgment was not mitigated by events in 2003, as Bush's push toward war culminated in the invasion of Iraq in late March. Leading Democrats, Old and New, supported the invasion and raised only sporadic criticism of the administration's obvious hyping of the Iraq weapons of mass destruction threat and the dubious intelligence that lay behind it. Once more, it seemed to Newer Democrats that all factions of the party were united in their ineffectiveness.

In late May, another round of tax cuts squeaked through Congress, with the Democrats putting up somewhat more resistance but still unable to stop the disciplined Republicans from pushing the cuts through. The new cuts brought the total cost of Bush's tax cuts to around $3 trillion over the course of the decade.

Finally, in November, the GOP managed to push through a Medicare prescription drugs bill with the help of Ted Kennedy (again!). Kennedy had been promised that the final bill would reflect Democratic concerns embodied in the more generous and consumer-friendly Senate bill he helped pass. However, Democrats with those concerns were systematically excluded by the Republican leadership from the reconciliation process. As a result, the final bill almost exclusively reflected the GOP approach—less generous and zealously protective of the pharmaceutical companies' prerogatives—embodied in the House bill.

On the side, GOP leaders like Tom DeLay were instigating Republican legislatures in Texas (successfully), Colorado (unsuccessfully), and other states to redraw Congressional boundaries to make the states more favorable to electing Republicans. Coming right after the standard redistricting based on the decennial census, this move to re-redistrict states went beyond accepted political norms and practices and was one more signal to Democrats that the contemporary GOP recognized no limits in its drive for political power.

These events led many (mostly younger) Democrats, or Newer Democrats, to respond to the party's challenges, not by picking or switching factional sides but by creating new institutions and developing new approaches that built on the Clinton synthesis of the 1990s to take on the Republican Party of the 2000s. In their view, there was simply no other way to go if the Democrats were to win in the future. The following are some examples of the new institutions and approaches that developed in the 2001–2003 period.

The Democratic Blogosphere. Pioneered by Markos Moulitsas Zúniga of Daily Kos, Jerome Armstrong of MyDD, and Joshua Micah Marshall of Talking Points Memo, Democratic weblogs, or "blogs," have grown exponentially since 2002, in terms of both readership and influence. The Daily Kos blog alone now registers well over 100,000 visits a day, and the initial pioneers have been joined by literally thousands more. Among them, they reach a Democratic audience of millions with a lively, opinionated mix of up-to-the-minute news, media criticism, poll results, electoral analyses, and anything else that seems politically relevant and interesting.

MoveOn.org. Whereas Democrats must come to visit the blogs and online magazines, MoveOn.org comes to visit Democrats. Founded in 1998 by software entrepreneurs Wes Boyd and Joan Blades to fight the Clinton impeachment drive of the right, the organization functions primarily via email and email-driven activist gath-

erings ("MeetUps") to solicit contributions for progressive and
Democratic causes, organize nonelectoral and electoral campaigns, and
communicate anti-Republican political news. The organization now
has more than 2 million members, and though still associated with
protest politics and grassroots lobbying (on issues ranging from the
Iraq war to media deregulation), it has moved increasingly into Democratic electoral politics.

The Dean Campaign and Internet Fundraising. Until late January
2004, the big news in the campaign for the Democratic nomination
was the spectacular rise of Howard Dean. He came out of nowhere
in 2003 to dominate the nomination race, leading in most state polls
and critically far outdistancing his Democratic rivals in fundraising.
Dean's campaign raised $40 million in 2003 from 280,000 individ-
uals making an average contribution of $143. Almost all of this fund-
raising was done over the Internet. As Noam Scheiber of the *New
Republic* pointed out,[14] the secret of the Dean campaign's success was
figuring out that the Internet could be used to radically decrease the
"cost per body" for a candidate seeking the nomination. In the past,
candidates had to knock on doors, make phone calls, or send mail
(and do it over and over again) to round up their supporters. With
the Dean campaign's methods, it was possible to generate supporters
at quite a low cost—indeed, the campaign came out ahead of the
game because one of the ways it organized these supporters was by
getting them to contribute money online. In so doing, the campaign
also mined these supporters for enthusiastic volunteers and generated
a "movement" level of energy at the grassroots of the Democratic
Party. That all this could be done so cheaply and quickly using the
Internet and Internet-driven MeetUps was a signal to Newer Democrats that they were on the right track. This was something that

14. Noam Scheiber, "Organization Man: Joe Trippi Reinvents Campaigning,"
New Republic, November 17, 2003.

New Democrats or New Old Democrats would never have thought of.

The Democratic 527s.   There has been an amazing proliferation of Democratic-oriented 527s (the name comes from the section of the tax code under which they fall), created to get around the McCain-Feingold law's prohibition on soft money. These independent groups are launching huge get-out-the-vote drives, using their own elaborate targeting databases, as well as arranging massive buys of television ads to slam Bush and support John Kerry in the 2004 election. Some forty groups plan to spend more than $300 million in these efforts.

Center for American Progress.   The Center for American Progress (CAP) was founded in the last half of 2003, with John Podesta, former Clinton chief of staff, as CEO and backed by about $10 million in contributions from wealthy Democrats like George Soros. By the spring of 2004, CAP had moved to a prominent, if not dominant, position among Democratic-leaning think tanks, eclipsing both the labor-liberal Economic Policy Institute and the New Democrat's Progressive Policy Institute.

What all these institutions and approaches have in common is a pragmatic Newer Democrat commitment to taking the Democratic Party as it actually is today—with the new coalition and the new vision of progressivism that has evolved over more than thirty years—and making it into a winning electoral instrument. Newer Democrats are *consolidating* a transformation of the Democratic Party instead of trying to launch a new one or fighting old battles in the manner of the DLC.

As the Democratic campaign has taken shape in 2004, it is easy to see how the Newer Democrat approach is influencing it. First, it's worth noting that neither the orthodox New Democrat Joe Lieberman nor the venerable New Old Democrat candidate Dick Gephardt ever developed any political traction; thus, both had to bow out of the race early. Wes Clark and John Edwards, who were not clearly beholden to either party faction, lasted longer. And the victor, John Kerry, from the very beginning of his campaign, had strong backers from both wings of the party and consciously steered away from being either side's candidate. As a result, Kerry enjoys wide support from all segments of the party and takes an exceptionally unified Democratic Party into the general election.

Kerry has also successfully adopted Dean-style Internet fundraising. Within forty-eight hours of Super Tuesday, March 2, when Kerry wrapped up the nomination, he had raised $4.6 million online. The money continued to pour in throughout March, helping Kerry raise an amazing $43 million for the month and $57 million for first quarter of the year, a presidential fundraising record. By the end of the second quarter, Kerry's fundraising had hit the astonishing total of $182 million, putting him within shouting distance of President Bush's fundraising total, something political professionals had initially believed was impossible. This money is in addition to the money that will be spent on his behalf by the 527s. In March and April of 2004 alone, the 527s spent about $28 million in the battleground states, attacking Bush as sort of an opening salvo in their campaign. The online Democratic Party—MoveOn and the Democratic blogosphere—is also fully mobilized on Kerry's behalf, directing their considerable energies against Bush and for Kerry and his campaign.

Kerry's policy and thematic approach reflect an effort to build on and extend the Clinton synthesis. He blends a consistently populist rhetoric with a moderate economic approach that emphasizes both deficit reduction and new spending on health care, jobs, and education. On foreign policy, he puts forward nuanced views (too nuanced, for some) that combine a willingness to use military force with the need to build international coalitions against terrorism and other threats. He has also avoided becoming entangled in divisive social issues like gun control and gay marriage, emphasizing his personal passion for hunting and his support for traditional marriage. None of this is to say, of course, that he has solved the problem of, say, reconciling Robert Rubin–style economics with increased social spending. But solving that kind of problem rather than favoring one side or another of these long-running debates is clearly his intent.

Other signs abound that the 2004 Democratic campaign will illustrate the increasing irrelevance of the New Democrat–New Old Democrat divide. The New Democrat Network (NDN), a DLC spin-off that was originally supposed to function as the organization's political action committee, has now clearly departed from its parent organization's politics. NDN's president, Simon Rosenberg, has committed his organization to promoting the Dean campaign's methods of organizing and fundraising and works closely with Daily Kos founder Zúniga. Indeed, when the Dean campaign was in its ascendancy and DLC leaders were excoriating Dean for leading the party down the path to Mondale-McGovernism and certain ruin, Rosenberg pointedly refused to make those criticisms and concentrated instead on praising the Dean campaign for its organizing innovations. In general, Rosenberg and his organization seem to have lost interest in the intraparty polemics that still animate DLC leaders.

However, even the DLC leaders are softening their approach, as they perceive the decreasing likelihood that a factional defense of New Democrat principles will yield much political influence. Will Marshall remarked earlier in 2004 that "we are all populists now," thanks, he said, to the need to oppose Bush's "crony capitalism." Given that this statement came from the leader of an organization that had invested considerable energy in denouncing populism throughout its history, particularly after the 2000 election, there was undoubtedly more to this admission than Marshall was willing to admit. Essentially, the market for orthodox New Democrat approaches has dried up, and the New Democrats are having to adapt to that reality.

New Old Democrats, for their part, are showing little interest in pressing Kerry to adopt a more forthrightly liberal/populist program. They are well aware of the New Democrat tinge to much of that program, but as Dick Gephardt put it once, "we are all New Democrats now." The New Old Democrats realize that if they hope to retain their influence in the party, they must accept the emphasis on winning and the de-emphasis on ideological debate, which are the hallmarks of the Newer Democrat approach. Indeed, in early 2004, moves were afoot to bury the hatchet with their New Democrat rivals by, among other things, publishing joint articles (for example, by Will Marshall and Robert Kuttner[15]) in the liberal-leaning *American Prospect* (now edited by Newer Democrat sympathizer Michael Tomasky).

It seems likely, however, that despite this moderation, New Old Democrats, like orthodox New Democrats, will continue to decline in influence. If not dead, they are certainly dying. Gephardt and Kennedy, the quintessential representatives of this tendency, have taken huge hits to their reputations in the past several years, and replacements of their stature are not obvious. This doesn't mean that the ideas and concerns of these Democrats will disappear, for they are intimate parts of the new vision of progressivism forged by the Clinton synthesis, but it is as *parts* of that synthesis that the New Old Democrats' ideas will endure. Their full-throated New Deal liberalism will never again be the dominant current of thought within the party.

15. Robert Kuttner and Will Marshall, "Come Together," *American Prospect*, June 2004.

CHAPTER TWO

Cotton on the roadside, cotton in the ditch.
We all picked the cotton but we never got rich.
Daddy was a veteran, a southern Democrat.
They oughta get a rich man to vote like that.

Well somebody told us Wall Street fell
But we were so poor that we couldn't tell.
Cotton was short and the weeds were tall
But Mr. Roosevelt's agonna save us all.

Well momma got sick and daddy got down.
The county got the farm and they moved to town.
Papa got a job with the TVA.
He bought a washing machine and then a Chevrolet.

    —Bob McDill, "Song of the South,"
      on Alabama, *Southern Star* (1989)

The Old and New Democratic Parties

Thomas Byrne Edsall

OVER THE PAST seventy-plus years, the American progressive tradition has changed radically. In its triumphant years, roughly from 1932 to 1966, a liberal Democratic agenda was developed to expand access to the middle class, to promote international trade, and to deploy government spending, all to foster full employment. The New Deal coalition was, in its essence, an economically based alliance of the ascendant.

The underlying moral premise of the Democratic Party of the Roosevelt era was that government constituted an essential force for the prevention of economic catastrophe and social inequity. Looking back over his first term, Franklin Roosevelt described the role of government:

> We of the Republic sensed the truth that democratic government has innate capacity to protect its people against disasters once considered inevitable, to solve problems once considered unsolvable. We would not admit that we could not find a way to master economic epidemics just as, after centuries of fatalistic suffering, we had found a way to master epidemics of disease. We refused to leave the problems of our common welfare to be solved by the

winds of chance and the hurricanes of disaster. . . . We have begun
to bring private autocratic powers into their proper subordination
to the public's government. The legend that they were invincible—
above and beyond the processes of a democracy—has been shattered. They have been challenged and beaten.[1]

The New Deal agenda entailed a massive expansion of the federal
government into the domestic sphere, an expansion configured explicitly around the goal of security, the regulation of financial institutions,
the forced accountability of business, a degree of federally imposed
redistribution, and government-supervised wage and employment
practices.

Major New Deal initiatives created procedures and mechanisms
to oversee the generation of wealth and to protect the rights of workers. Hallmark measures included the Federal Emergency Relief Program, the Emergency Banking Act of 1933, the Federal Deposit
Insurance Corporation, the Securities and Exchange Commission, the
Social Security Administration, the Rural Electrification Administration, the National Industrial Recovery Act of 1933, the Civilian Conservation Corps, the Works Progress Administration, the National
Labor Relations Act of 1936, the Fair Labor Standards Act of 1938
(including the first minimum wage), and so forth.

During the New Deal era, "liberalism" conveyed to most Americans a right to economic safeguards and the tempering of market
forces through the power of government action. In the years since
1966, liberalism has undergone a major conceptual transformation,
and its adherents have splintered into two factions. The first of these
factions is made up of an alliance of the so-called subdominant, who
are joined by the shared goal of seeking a haven from market pressures
as well as insulation from majoritarian moral and social norms that
are often experienced as discriminatory. This alliance includes within

---

1. Franklin D. Roosevelt, Second Inaugural Address, Wednesday, January 20,
1937, http://www.bartleby.com/124/pres50.html.

it (1) the victims of economic competition—low-wage workers, the unemployed, and the unemployable—and those without the skills to prevail in the postindustrial economy; (2) racial, ethnic, and other minorities historically barred from social and economic participation; and (3) those seeking government support in the aftermath of the cultural revolutions of the past forty years, which have led to divorce and nonmarital birth rates that often leave single women and children in need of the basic necessities of life. The focus on rights for such subordinated groups—including the disabled, the aged, the addicted, and the mentally ill rather than for the entire working class or for all the have-nots—has produced new schisms within the Democratic Party.

Adding to the volatility of the contemporary Democratic coalition has been a second major faction made up of highly educated voters, frequently in professions that require advanced degrees. Over the past four decades, the conversion of professionals (variously known as the "knowledge class," the "new class," "information workers," or "symbol analysts") to a solid base for the Democrats has helped compensate in numbers for the defection of skilled and semiskilled lower-income white workers to the GOP. From 1960 to the present, the percentage of Democratic presidential voters employed in the professions has doubled, from 18 to 35 percent, whereas the share of the Democratic vote made up of lower-income skilled and nonskilled workers has dropped from 50 percent to 35 percent.[2]

As the political and economic liberalism of the New Deal era has been transformed, it has lost the unambiguous majority support of middle- and lower-income white voters—voters who adhere to values oriented toward discipline rather than nurturance, or to use another formulation, discipline versus therapy.[3] This cultural chasm has, over

2. Jeff Manza and Clem Brooks, *Social Cleavages and Policy Change: Voter Alignments and U.S. Party Coalitions* (Oxford University Press, 1999), 190–94, 232–38.
3. Thomas B. Edsall, "Two Areas Reflect Deep Divide," *Washington Post*, April 13, A1.

the past four decades, pitted a progressive and highly educated elite within the Democratic Party against less-affluent Democratic cultural conservatives who oppose abortion, same-sex marriage, and busing, and who, in general, defend traditional gender roles and conventional social mores.

Knowledge workers with postsecondary degrees are not voting Democratic to advance their economic interests, as did trade unionists, European immigrants, urban Catholics, rural whites, and newly enfranchised blacks during the heyday of the twentieth-century Democratic Party. Indeed, the knowledge-worker class often espouses values and beliefs adversarial to America's business enterprises, mounting critiques of corporate greed and profiteering. Instead, the central political motivation of the new Democratic professional class has been to support a politics that reflects its beliefs in a range of recently democratized rights centered on autonomy, self-development, and individualism. Although such voters do not seek pork-barrel benefits from the government, they do seek government funding of programs consistent with their ideological commitments—for example, government affirmation and enforcement of such key rights as women's rights, the right to sexual privacy, the right to self-expression, the right to agreed-upon race and gender preferences, and the right to claim once-stigmatized identities like homosexuality. In addition, upscale Democratic activists focus on environmental issues, antiglobalization, freedom of artistic expression (films, lyrics, television or radio programming, Internet content, etc.), and ideological support for tolerance of difference and for a broadly conceived multiculturalism.

Since the 1960s, as the country's affluence has increased, this knowledge class has become a powerful force within the Democratic Party—from Hollywood to university communities to the world of cosmopolitan professionals—shaping, and shaped by, the civil rights, antiwar, feminist, and gay rights movements, as well as by the broader sexual and information revolutions. Members of this class fought for, and had their lives transformed by, decades of technological innovation and have a history of success at social reform: forcing the withdrawal of American troops from Vietnam, abolishing the military draft, legalizing contraception and abortion, allowing no-fault divorce, toppling the Nixon administration, effectively eradicating censorship, and preserving the nation's forests, wildlife, seashores, mountain ranges, and endangered species. Activists also worked to limit the use of force by attempting to abolish the death penalty; to curb police brutality, corporal punishment, domestic abuse, and the proliferation of nuclear weapons; and to reduce the frequency and lethality of war.

The conflation of social-cultural and economic-technological-scientific upheavals over the past four decades has brought a whole new set of values, objectives, and cross pressures into the Democratic Party, creating friction with voters disoriented and angered by accelerating social change and suffering an acute sense of status-displacement—voters to whom traditional patriotic and religious beliefs serve as a bedrock. The new focus of upper-income Democrats on self-actualization, nonviolence, and aesthetic needs have conflicted, in many ways, with the needs of the less-privileged—those feeling more victmized than empowered by contemporary cultural trends. These less-privileged voters put a premium on continuity and familiarity and often couple an antimodernist bias with a central focus on economic and physical security, as well as on work and entry into the middle class rather than on less concrete postmaterialist rights or identity goals.

In contrast, the upscale cohort within the Democratic coalition is intensely hostile to agendas of imposed moral orthodoxy, particularly to the agenda of the Christian Right. Whereas knowledge workers have increasingly come to see the Republican Party as moralistic and culturally intrusive and, as such, a threat to personal freedom, sizeable numbers of middle- to lower-income white voters see moral and religious orthodoxies as reassuring, stabilizing, and politically attractive. The Democratic Party is attempting to straddle this values gap, but it is in persistent danger of disturbing the fragile equilibrium between its donor base and some of its most crucial voting blocs.

The Demise of the New Deal Coalition

To a significant extent, the successes of the New Deal coalition have spelt its demise. In 1940, Roosevelt referred to one-third of the nation as "ill-clothed, ill-housed, ill-fed."[4] Today, that proportion has shrunk to 12.1 percent, while the standards by which we define poverty have risen sharply.[5] In 1940, more than half of the U.S. population had completed no more than an eighth-grade education. In 1992, 48.9 percent of 25- to 29-year-olds reported completing some college.[6] The more privileged among workers have become stockholders and stake-holders. Renters have become property owners. The upper strata of the have-nots have become haves, with much to conserve and with newly hungry competitors to guard against. The ethnic enmity among northern and southern, or Catholic and Protestant, European immi-grants, which was characteristic of Democratic and Republican rival-ries in the first half of the twentieth century, has given way to a pan-European identity in the face of a large population influx from non-European countries.

As members of the working class represented by strong unions in the 1950s, 1960s, and early 1970s became middle class, and as sub-urban homeowners with high wages, extensive benefits, and secure pensions lost their sense of economic oppression, motivation to join

4. Franklin D. Roosevelt, Radio Address at the White House Conference on Children in a Democracy, January 19, 1940, http://www.presidency.ucsb.edu/site/docs/pppus.php?admin=032&year=1940&id=9.

5. Bureau of the Census, "Poverty, Income See Slight Changes; Child Poverty Rate Unchanged, Census Bureau Reports," September 26, 2003, http://www.census.gov/Press-Release/www/2003/cb03-153.html.

6. National Center for Education Statistics, "Literacy from 1870 to 1979: Edu-cational Attainment," http://nces.ed.gov/naal/historicaldata/edattain.asp; National Center for Education Statistics, "Supplemental Note 2: The Current Population Survey," http://nces.ed.gov/programs/coe/2004/notes/n02.asp.

a biracial center-left coalition diminished. The civil rights revolution and the commitment of the Democratic Party to legal equality for African Americans produced new strains—pitting blacks, Hispanics, and upscale white liberals against white working- and lower-middle-class voters and splintering core elements of the party of the Left. As less well-off whites were forced to cede status, resources, and opportunities to new entrants from once-segregated populations, many dropped out of the Democratic Party altogether.

Even as the economic liberalism of the New Deal era has waned and as cultural liberalism has become more prominent within the Democratic Party, however, there is always the possibility of a new Democratic coalition sufficiently strong enough to challenge, and perhaps defeat, the current Republican alliance. This is particularly so if the party machinery, aspiring candidates, and primary voters can coordinate a reconfiguration that addresses the party's historical weakness on issues of culture, mainstream values, and national defense. If they are able to do so, the underpinnings and the guiding agenda of this new Democratic majority would likely radically pare the ambitious redistributive economic aims of the Democratic Party of the past.

The Rise and Fall of Organized Labor

No institution better illustrates the transformation of the political Left than organized labor. During the middle decades of the twentieth century, the union movement in America was on the way up. It became a powerful force in those private-sector industries that grew massively in the wake of the Second World War: automobiles, steel, the construction trades, trucking, and shipbuilding. Union leaders and members were overwhelmingly male, and they used their muscle to shut down factories and building sites to force steady gains in wages and benefits.

The share of the private-sector workforce represented by organized labor nearly tripled between 1930 and 1960, skyrocketing from 13.3

percent to 37 percent as unions became an integral and powerful part of America's free enterprise system.[7] Union leaders were themselves aggressive and dominant figures—Walter Reuther of the United Auto Workers, John L. Lewis of the United Mine Workers, Jimmy Hoffa of the Teamsters, Harry Bridges of the International Longshoremen's Union, and George Meany, the plumber who rose to the presidency of the AFL-CIO.

During this period, not only were unions becoming stronger, but also the labor movement as a whole powered mobility, as millions of workers moved up the social scale. The central purpose of unions, the Democratic Party, and political liberalism in this period was to steadily improve the socioeconomic status for the entire working class. The government-backed institutions of the New Deal—in tandem with social innovations of the Second World War, such as the GI Bill— were put in place by Democratic majorities and were designed, either directly or indirectly, to help workers and farmers earn a decent return on their labor, for veterans to get a college education, for widows and a small number of abandoned women to get support for their children, and for the elderly to receive a reliable subsistence income.

Concomitant with the sociocultural movements of the early 1970s, and linked to the technological revolutions of the postwar era (computerization, mechanization, and telecommunications), the character and composition of the trade union movement began to change. Most important, organized labor began to implode in the private sector, as global competition prompted American corporations to begin a major assault against employees whose pay and benefit packages had abruptly become a competitive liability in the face of low production costs overseas.

Private sector union leaders were no longer able to face CEOs as equals across the bargaining table. Rather, unions suddenly found

---

7. For growth in unionized workforce, Bureau of Labor Statistics, http://www.bls.gov/.

themselves struggling simply to survive, burdened by growing obligations to provide modest benefits to the ranks of the non–dues paying, unemployed members. "We went from being the tough guys on the block to being social workers handing out food to laid off workers," said steelworker organizer and lobbyist John J. "Jack" Sheehan.[8]

Private-sector unions were no longer ascendant, aggressive, or dominant. The percentage of the private-sector workforce represented by labor unions fell from the high of 37 percent in 1960 to just 8.2 percent by 2003, the lowest level since at least 1905.[9] This decline in private-sector union membership has been accompanied by two additional, politically significant trends: the growth of public-sector (government) union membership and the steady decline in the number of men represented by unions.

In 1976, when private-sector unionization was starting its decline, government workers in labor unions represented only 16.7 percent of all union members. By 2003, organized government workers represented nearly half (46.2 percent) of the union movement. Male membership, in turn, declined from 82.7 percent of union members in 1960 to 58.4 percent in 2001. In sheer numbers, there were 12.4 million male union members in 1960; in 2003, there were 9.0 million, or 3.48 million fewer. During these forty-three years, the total number of men in the workforce grew by 19.9 million, from 43.4 million to 63.3 million.[10] Conversely, the percentage of women in the union movement grew from 17.3 percent in 1960 to 42.7 percent in 2003; women will soon make up the majority of union members. The United Auto Workers noted in 2002 that all of the labor move-

---

8. Jack Sheehan, interview with author, 1988.

9. Department of Labor, Bureau of Labor Statistics, Union Membership Annual Report 2004, available at http://www.bls.gov/news.release/union2.toc.htm.

10. Bureau of Labor Statistics, Table 1. Union affiliation of employed wage and salary workers by selected characteristics, http://www.bls.gov/news.release/union2.t01.htm.

ment's net membership gain in 2001 was among women: male union membership fell by 76,000, but female membership increased by 93,000.[11]

What the data about organized labor demonstrate is how crucially this institutional base of the Democratic Party has changed over the past four decades. Organized labor has shifted from an overwhelmingly male movement with the genuine power to make demands and to shut down whole industries—a dominant and dynamic presence on the American scene—to a movement in decline, heavily dependent on tax dollars to pay the wages and benefits of its public-sector membership. "We have gone from a movement in which the primary skill was managing success to a movement fighting to stay alive," commented Andrew L. Stern, president of the Service Employees International Union, now the second largest in the AFL-CIO.[12]

The once-proud private sector unions—the United Auto Workers, the Teamsters, the Steelworkers, and the Ironworkers—were, from the 1930s through the 1960s, allied with their employers in support of competitive free trade policies and confident in their ability to produce better goods than their foreign competitors produce. Today these same unions, and many of their employers, are proponents of various forms of trade protectionism, seeking to insulate themselves from the now serious threat of foreign cars, steel, textiles, and other capital goods. The shift in the stance toward trade regulation is a direct result of the shift in the U.S. economy from net exporter of manufactured goods to net importer. At the same time, by the mid-1990s, roughly 37 percent of union members had become sufficiently alienated from the cultural imperatives of the new Democratic Party that they began voting Republican—first in presidential elections and then in congressional elections.[13]

11. Ibid.
12. Andrew Stern, interview with the author, March 2003.
13. In the 2000 presidential election, 37 percent of voters in union households voted for George W. Bush, according to Voters News Service (VNS) Exit Polls, http://www.cnn.com/ELECTION/2000/epolls/US/P000.html.

The Evolving Post-1965 Coalition

The redistributive liberalism of the New Deal era had resulted in a unique achievement: it forged a coalition in which most, but by no means all, constituents were located in the bottom half of American society. This alliance of the economically disadvantaged was achieved by a political strategy and a legislative agenda that endorsed, and did not violate, received social norms—including conventional family organization and religious observance. School prayer and the Ten Commandments were ubiquitous. Everyday patriotism, a reverence for the flag, obligatory military service, deference toward hierarchy, a traditional work and achievement ethic, the materialistic ambitions of working people, and the Horatio Alger dimension to the lived experience of many Americans held undisputed sway among the vast majority of Democratic Party adherents. This alliance was forged, moreover, with full acceptance of the hard rules of politics: that winners win and losers lose; that winning elections creates power; and that such victories, and the power thus achieved, create opportunity. In the case of the New Deal coalition, this provided a means for millions of once-poor Americans to set their sights on material prosperity—to buy a home, a car, and an education for their children that would assure the next generation of better lives.

As noted, this coalition's success brought about its own decline: growing numbers of citizens entered the middle class, moved to the suburbs, acquired houses, and earned the right to higher levels of schooling, and their self-identification inevitably shifted away from the have-nots. Aspirations toward higher social status and new goals of self-realization spread rapidly. At the same time, by the 1960s and 1970s, leaders of the Democratic coalition accelerated the weakening of their party by failing to manage the growing salience of emerging and divisive issues: issues of race and rights, including civil rights, reproductive rights (including the new technologies of oral contraception and surgical abortion), criminal defendants' rights (coupled with escalating rates of crime), and welfare rights, as well as of conflicts over time posed by use of force in places as remote as Southeast Asia, Nicaragua, the Balkans, and the Middle East.

Conflicts within the party also erupted between, on the one hand, a massive youthful demographic of expressive individualists—the Doctor Spock generation—who were heavily influenced by ideals of the therapeutic and of freedom from the shackles of social subordination, and, on the other hand, the more discipline-oriented, traditionally patriotic, "silent majority," who were committed to honoring and conserving treasured customs and forms. At the same time, the role of government in all of these volatile issues was amplified and driven home by steadily rising tax burdens, with government revenues channeled into policies and programs inevitably reflecting culturally liberal values.

In sum, leaders of, and activists within, the liberal coalition failed to foresee and to adequately manage the dangers posed by the fusion of issues configured around liberation, race, and rights—and the burden imposed by new levels of taxation—and the way in which these issues could and did turn key New Deal constituencies into adversaries of what came simply to be called liberalism—the infamous L-word against which Ronald Reagan and George H. W. Bush campaigned so successfully throughout the 1980s.

The shift in the liberal agenda from a focus on broad economic advancement for those in the bottom half of the income distribution to the granting of and protection of rights for specific interest groups allowed both Reagan and the first Bush to use liberalism as a wedge issue, designed to break the Democratic loyalties of more socially conservative working- and lower-middle-class white voters—the voters who became known throughout the 1980s as Reagan Democrats.

From 1962 to 1980, by failing to adjust tax rates in response to escalating inflation and in response to rising incomes due to the entry of married women into the workforce—a development that forced middle-income families into tax brackets originally designed to capture only the well-to-do—Democratic-controlled Congresses allowed the burden of the progressive marginal rates in the income tax to increasingly fall on the moderate-income voters who were essential to the maintenance of a liberal majority coalition. During this period, the marginal tax rate (the tax on the last dollar earned) for all taxpayers rose from 24.5 percent to 32.2 percent, roughly a 30 percent increase.[14] Similarly, the average tax rate (the rate on all income) rose from 12.8 to 15.9 percent, a roughly 25 percent increase.[15]

Just as Democrats were imposing rising taxes on their own base, making it increasingly costly for taxpayers to support government spending that benefited previously disenfranchised groups, the agenda of the Democratic Party shifted from the universal programs of the New Deal and the Fair Deal to a focus on benefits for members of minority groups—first legal equality through civil rights legislation, then economic opportunity through affirmative action, then expanded services and payments to children born out of wedlock, and then subsidized jobs programs for unmarried fathers. Policies adopted by the federal government to redistribute benefits to African Americans—morally unambiguous in the eyes of many, if not most, voters as an appropriate redress for centuries of slavery—were steadily expanded to encompass other disadvantaged minorities. These other minorities were often voluntary migrants to the United States, or their descendants, who had deliberately sought entry to this country and who had not, in the view of many, been legally discriminated against.

This expansion of civil rights legislation originally designed for African Americans to encompass groups including women, the elderly, Hispanics, Pacific Islanders, gays, and those embroiled in the criminal justice system—from death row inmates to recreational drug users—resulted from two parallel developments: first, the need of civil rights

14. Eugene Steurerle and Michael Hartzmark, "Individual Income Taxation: 1947–1979," Office of Tax Analysis, Department of the Treasury, undated, copy supplied to author by Eugene Steurele.

15. Ibid.

leaders to gain new allies in legislative and court battles, and, second, the growing assertiveness and strength of groups representing such large populations as Hispanics, women, and the elderly. The leaders of these groups often found that the rights and preferences granted African Americans were attractive as a means of addressing the demands of their own constituents. A series of Supreme Court decisions buttressed by lower courts as well as by actions of the federal regulatory system, shaped policies determining who would get hired, who would get promoted, and who would get accepted to college and to graduate school in both the public and the private sector. These judicial, legislative, and regulatory developments were advocated by the platforms of the Democratic Party, although such policies would have had difficultly gaining either congressional approval or popular support.

The legal decisions that formed the foundation of the rights revolutions resulted, in part, from the purposeful use of the courts by minority groups, women's organizations, and others seeking to expand the rights agenda in the face of rising legislative and White House hostility, beginning in the 1970s. Such judicial and regulatory decisions, as well as new policies favoring migrants to the United States from developing countries (under the aegis of immigration reform enacted in the mid-1960s and supported by Democratic legislative majorities), had an immense impact on the lives of countless citizens, creating a vast pool of beneficiaries who developed loyalty to the party of government activism. But they also created a vast pool of those who felt unsettled and victimized by the arrival of these newcomers and who developed allegiance to the GOP as the party committed to reduced government intrusion.

For the leadership of the Democratic Party, the moral imperative of lowering barriers that had historically impeded access to opportunity for African Americans, women, and other disenfranchised groups was inescapable. At the same time, however, acceding to this imperative made holding together a biracial or multiethnic center-left majority coalition, with an equal number of male and female adherents, increasingly difficult, imposing choices and trade-offs that inevitably produced friction, hostility, and defectors, as well as new adherents.

By allowing tax burdens on white working- and lower-middle-class voters to rise, just as those voters perceived that the government they were paying for was intervening, at their expense, to allocate benefits to groups other than their own, Democrats invited the backlash that toppled the party—and the New Deal variant of liberalism—in the elections of 1968, 1972, 1980, 1984, 1988, and 2000, as well as in the midterm elections of 1994 (the year of the "angry white male," when Democrats finally lost both the House and the Senate).

The costs of the rights revolution fell most heavily on working-class whites, as unions, police forces, fire departments, and all levels of government and civil service employment, in addition to jobs within large private corporations subject to federal regulation, were opened to previously discriminated against and otherwise barred competitors. Schools in once all-white neighborhoods became subject to court-ordered hiring goals, as well as to court-ordered multilingual and other special-education programs, creating new groups of enraged or gratified voters. At the same time, however, more affluent white neighborhood schools in the suburbs and in rapidly growing exurbia remained relatively untouched, as did the professional lives of many doctors, lawyers, journalists, academics, and other workers at the more privileged levels of the information economy, who still enjoyed the relatively insular comforts of upper-middle-class life.

Democratic leaders were faced with what, even in retrospect, seemed an insoluble dilemma: How was the party to alleviate competition for scarce resources, both tangible and intangible, such as jobs, pay increases, classroom time, slots in universities, space in the literary canon, and other matters of cultural authority and prestige? Competition was often tinged with deeply felt convictions concerning justice—dissension between those committed to the rights of criminal perpetrators who had suffered childhood poverty and abuse—and those committed to the rights of the victims of crime. How was the party of the common man to reconcile the interests of white South Boston and black Roxbury, or white south St. Louis and black north St. Louis? How could it offer the right to instruction in their native tongue to the more than thirty language groups registered in schools clustered around the nation's largest cities? Indeed, how could the party produce the wherewithal to feed the seemingly insatiable appetite for opportunity, benefits, and government services of a rapidly democratizing, multiethnic, multicultural citizenry endowed with certain loosely specified inalienable rights?

In practice, by the mid-1960s, Democrats had embarked on large-scale programs of social reform, including health care for the poor, welfare for an exploding population of single mothers, special education for the legions of learning disabled, nutritional programs for inner-city infants and children, Spanish-language signage in public buildings, and so forth. These programs committed tax revenues that were widely viewed by lower- and middle-income whites as being weighted toward "another" America. Ronald Reagan captured the sentiments of many of these voters when he declared, as he did so often, "I didn't leave the Democratic Party, the party left me."

By the 1970s, Democratic Party platforms began to endorse nontraditional family structures. The sexual revolution, the women's movement, antiwar protestors, and the student counterculture all served to radicalize previously quiescent sectors of the American populace, to increase competitive pressures for limited resources, and to compound the difficulties of those seeking to maintain the remnants of the majority Left coalition, even while providing substantial new populations of beneficiaries and adherents for the Left. Many of the insurgents within the Democratic Party during this period, especially those traveling the route from the student Left to the upper councils of the Democratic Party, conveyed contempt for the materialistic values of union members and traditional middle-American constituencies—the goal of a quarter-acre lot, a tract house, a two-car garage, a ride-on mower, a power boat, and a cabin by the shore. At the same time, the new "elitism" at the upper levels of the Democratic Party attracted substantial numbers of upper-income voters who felt more at home in the left coalition as its culture became more intellectually sophisticated and compatible with their own views.

In effect, an elite cultural progressivism in many ways supplanted the Democratic Party's economic progressivism of the 1930s, 1940s, 1950s, and early 1960s. The two-parent family with a male head of household lost its privileged position within the social order; indeed, it was often demonized by the new Left as an institution of patriarchal oppression. Even as this attitudinal shift alienated those with "bourgeois" family values, it attracted new antitraditionalists, such as sexual libertarians, vast numbers of unmarried women, and so on.

In addition, the historic economic class divisions of the New Deal period were augmented by a range of movements, often jostling uncomfortably under the standard of the Democratic Party. New configurations of support and opposition emerged regarding the introduction of laws regulating novel reproductive technologies, sexual harassment, child support and custody disputes, violence against women, and sexual harassment. Such shifts from a center-left political alliance based on economic status to one based not only on economic concerns but also on broadly conceived human rights, as well as on cultural identity and affinity, resulted in growing divisions within Democratic ranks. A socially liberal, well-educated, secular Left leadership cohort joined forces with racial minorities, unwed mothers, gay rights activists, and other previously marginalized groups. They opposed a Republican Party funded and led by the very wealthy and by a corporate ownership and managerial class, which sought a reduction in the regulatory and tax burdens of big government and which allied with a culturally conservative, religiously observant, materialistic white working and lower middle class seeking to stem the tax-fueled and government-sponsored tides of change.

The congressional elections of 1966 first demonstrated the vulnerability of the splintering New Deal coalition, when Democrats lost 44 House seats in the wake of the Civil Rights Act of 1964, the 1965 riot in the African American Watts section of Los Angeles, the 1966 race riots in Chicago, and reports of sharply rising crime rates in virtually every region of the nation. The 1968 independent presidential bids of both Eugene McCarthy on the left and Alabama governor George C. Wallace on the right magnified this vulnerability. The Wallace bid proved particularly prophetic. Wallace won 13 percent of the popular vote and forty-six electoral college votes from the states of the Deep South in a campaign that both defended segregation and portrayed the Democratic Party as an elitist institution imposing on America not only forced integration but also the values of pointy-headed intellectuals.

Wallace's 1968 message was based on race, but its appeal extended far beyond to a larger "populism of the right." Wallace gave voice to the growing conviction of working- and middle-class white voters that their values, their neighborhoods, their ambitions, and their traditions were under assault by a powerful liberal elite that had extended its domination to Congress, to the courts, and to the leadership cadre of the Democratic Party. In his last presidential campaign in 1976, Wallace told voters, "We haven't been against people. We've been against big government trying to take over and write a guideline for you and tell you how to cross the street, what to do with your union and your business when you know how to do it yourself."[16]

In 1968, running as an independent candidate in the general election against Democratic nominee Hubert H. Humphrey and against Republican nominee Richard M. Nixon, Wallace declared: "It is a sad day in our country that you cannot walk even in your neighborhoods at night or even in the daytime because both national par-

16. Wallace quotes available on the Public Broadcasting Service website, at http://www.pbs.org/wgbh/amex/wallace/sfeature/quotes.html.

ties, in the last number of years, have kowtowed to every group of anarchists that have roamed the streets of San Francisco and Los Angeles and throughout the country. And now they have created themselves a Frankenstein monster, and the chickens are coming home to roost all over this country. . . . Yes, they've looked down their nose at you and me a long time. They've called us rednecks—the Republicans and the Democrats. Well, we're going to show, there sure are a lot of rednecks in this country."[17]

The Wallace constituency—enlarged over the subsequent quarter-century to encompass Richard M. Nixon's silent majority, the Reagan Democrats of 1980 and 1984, the disaffected males so influential in Newt Gingrich's Republican revolution of 1994, and the voters backing both presidents Bush—began as a renegade protest against the emerging shape of Democratic sociocultural and racial liberalism and has by now become a crucial Republican constituency. This constituency, more than any other, has been the single most important factor in American politics, from the congressional elections of 1966 to the midterm elections of 2002. This is not to minimize the significance of other constituencies in election outcomes—women, Hispanics, Blacks, Asians, gay rights activists, and many others have, and continue to, cast decisive votes. Women overall, for example, voted for Gore 54–43, while men voted for Bush 53–42. But, while working women voted for Gore by a 58–39 margin, nonworking women voted for Bush by a 52–44 margin, according to the Voter News Service 2000 exit polls.[18]

The complex center-left alliance may indeed, again, form an election-day majority, as it did in 2000 when Al Gore won the popular vote, but its margin has become so slender as to be in constant peril.

In an era dominated by the victories of the Republican Party—not only at the presidential but also at the congressional, gubernato-

17. Ibid.
18. 2000 Voter News Service (VNS) exit poll data, http://www.cnn.com/ELECTION/2000/results/index.president.html.

rial, and state-legislative levels—it is the group of white, moderate-income, disproportionately male voters behind the GOP that has most consistently exerted the leverage to propel American politics to the right. Successful Republican candidates—most notably Reagan and George W. Bush—have often adopted right-populist cadences and rhetoric—the "common touch" designed to reach and emotionally tap into the concerns of key voters on the middle and lower rungs of the social ladder. The party of commerce, industry, and wealth generation, the party of resistance to progressive taxes, government regulation, and government-funded social benefits, has found a crucial ally among overwhelmingly white working- and middle-class voters whose experience has led them to see much of what government visibly provides as adverse to their own most cherished interests.

Maintaining the Contemporary Coalition

The Democratic coalition, on the other hand, continues in many ways as a union of the have-nots. Economic divisions remain a significant factor in elections. Al Gore beat George Bush by 13 percentage points among voters making $15,000 to $30,000, according to exit polls by Voter News Service (VNS), while voters making more than $100,000 backed Bush over Gore by 11 points.[19]

There is now, however, a host of other factors that are significantly more predictive of voting behavior than income or education. The intensity of voters' religious convictions, measured by church attendance, is currently a much stronger indicator of partisan preference than is economic status. The 14 percent of voters who attend religious services more than once a week supported Bush over Gore by a decisive 27-point margin (63 to 36 percent). The 14 percent of voters who never go to church backed Gore over Bush by an even

19. Exit poll data available at the CNN website, http://www.cnn.com/ELECTION/2000/epolls/US/P000.html.

larger 29 points (61 to 32 percent).[20] In fact, the answers to public opinion surveys to questions on abortion, gun ownership, and even Hillary Clinton (as a proxy, arguably, for nontraditional roles for women) correlate much more strongly with voting behavior than a respondent's identification as a member of the working class or the upper middle class.[21]

Al Gore's 2000 campaign became a testing ground for advocates attempting to integrate the cultural liberalism of the modern Democratic Party with a renewed economic populism and a revitalized conception of a top versus bottom political contest. Democrats in 2000 painted the Bush campaign as financed by a new generation of special-interest power brokers who sought a pliant president who would bend public policy to suit their purposes and profits. The official theme of the Gore campaign became, "Standing up for the people, not the powerful." At the Democratic convention, Gore declared: "Whether you're in a suburb or an inner city, whether you raise crops or drive hogs and cattle on a farm, drive a big rig on the interstate or drive e-commerce on the Internet, whether you're starting out to raise your own family or getting ready to retire after a lifetime of hard work, so often powerful forces and powerful interests stand in your way, and the odds seem stacked against you, even as you do what's right for you and your family. . . . I want you to know this: I've taken on the powerful forces, and as president, I'll stand up to them and I'll stand up for you. . . . That's the difference in this election. They're for the powerful. We're for the people."[22]

Democratic pollster Stanley Greenberg, one of the principal architects of Gore's populist strategy, conducted a postelection survey to determine the effectiveness of Left-populist themes. His findings showed that Gore's campaign had done little or nothing to restore

20. Ibid.
21. Ibid.
22. Gore's acceptance speech is available at the CNN website, http://www.cnn.com/ELECTION/2000/conventions/democratic/transcripts/gore.html.

Democratic support among the key target constituencies of white men
and women without college degrees. The survey, conducted for the
Institute for America's Future (IAF), revealed that these constituencies
had significantly more positive feelings toward the Republican Party
than toward the Democratic Party. Asked whether their views were
warm or cool toward the two parties, white women without college
degrees were decisively favorable to the GOP (49 percent warm and
27 percent cool), while their assessment of the Democratic Party was
somewhat less positive (46 percent warm to 34 percent cool). For
noncollege white men, the differences were more dramatic: their positive view of the Republican Party was 54 percent to 27 percent, and
their assessment of the Democratic Party was negative, 38 percent to
41 percent.

In perhaps his most revealing finding, Greenberg told a gathering
of progressive activists sponsored by the IAF, "We lost it downscale
and gained it upscale. Progressives need to ask: What is the character
of a progressive movement without the aspiration to represent working-class voters?"[23]

Gore won a slim plurality of the vote with strong backing of
upscale white professional voters while failing to put together a sufficient popular majority to ensure an electoral college victory. This
failure was, in part, due to the defection to Bush of white working-
class voters, the original mainstay of the New Deal Democratic coalition. There is now, in fact, a contemporary progressive coalition,
but it has been transformed into a much more complex, difficult to
unite, and less reliable coalition.

The Republican coalition, of course, has its own major vulnerabilities. As the Christian Right and the antiabortion wing have gained
sway within the Republican Party, leading to the adoption of a strong
antiabortion plank, many secular voters, whose economic interests lie
with the GOP, have switched their allegiance to the party of the Left.

---

23. Poll data provided to the author by Stanley Greenberg.

In fact, secular voters are one of the fastest-growing populations in the United States, and such voters have a deep antipathy to the GOP's religious and moral conservatism. This shift has offered significant opportunities to the Left. The intensity and depth of the views of more secular voters has been demonstrated in repeated public poll findings showing majorities opposed to the impeachment of President Clinton and supporting Clinton, even in the aftermath of the Monica Lewinsky scandal.

The importance of the shift of these voters toward the Democratic coalition should not be underestimated. They are the driving force in the conversion of major suburban counties outside such coastal cities as New York, Philadelphia, and San Francisco from Republican bastions to increasingly reliable Democratic constituencies. Together with Hispanic voters, these contemporary voters have converted California from a leaning Republican state to a reliable source of electoral college votes for Democratic presidential candidates. Support for the right to an abortion has become a bedrock of support of the Democratic Party, and the abortion issue shows how the party has developed an issue strategy that does not comport with traditional economic populism. Among whites with high school diplomas or less, VNS exit polls taken in 2000 showed that a slight majority, 52 percent to 48 percent, believes that most abortions should be illegal. In contrast, whites with college and postgraduate degrees believe most abortions should be legal, by a resounding 63 percent to 37 percent.[24]

Issues revolving around violence constitute another noneconomic key to contemporary voter allegiance to the Democratic Party. Less well-educated whites are divided down the middle on this issue, whereas well-educated whites strongly support gun control, 66 percent to 34 percent.[25]

The emergence of dissonance as a key element within the center-

24. CNN, http://www.cnn.com/ELECTION/2000/epolls/US/P000.html.
25. Ibid.

left coalition is one of the primary reasons that the contemporary Democratic Party is so difficult to manage. A Democratic candidate, especially one seeking to win the presidency, must be able to develop a message—and, just as important, a tone—that joins the NAACP, NOW, La Raza, the Human Rights Campaign, Hollywood, the ACLU, AFSCME, and the AFL-CIO—bricklayers, government employees, laid-off steelworkers, and teachers. These groups must be united, just as an effective Republican candidate must pull together the support of key GOP constituencies—from Southern Baptists fearful of their now-porous communities to military personnel, ranchers, hedge-fund executives, hunters, and international currency traders—behind a banner of opposition to taxes, government regulation, and social spending; support for gun ownership; toleration of abridged civil liberties in the name of homeland defense; commitment to a military doctrine of preemptive war; belief in capital punishment; and devotion to traditional family values.

The Democratic coalition has been much harder to corral. Jimmy Carter won the 1976 election primarily in response to voter backlash against Watergate, but he proved unable to either master or manage Democratic congressional majorities on Capitol Hill or the competing wings of the party at large. Subsequently, he failed to win a second term. Clinton conducted a successful 1992 campaign but did not win a majority of the popular vote, as 19 percent of the electorate cast ballots for independent (and fiercely protectionist) candidate Ross Perot. Although Clinton laid the groundwork during his 1992 campaign for a more moderate Democratic coalition, promising to reverse what voters perceived as the cultural excesses of the Left—for example, by calling for a New Covenant on welfare—he crashed upon the shoals of the culture wars shortly after taking office.

Clinton's failure to lead his party back to the political center, as he had promised prior to his election, was evident on numerous fronts: his willingness to define his opening agenda in terms of abortion rights—the first executive order he signed upon assuming office was to permit, once again, abortion counseling in federally funded family planning programs; his "don't ask, don't tell" compromise regarding the service of gays in the military; and his delegation to his wife of the authority to reform national health policy. His actions angered the moderate voters who had backed him in 1992. They shifted in droves to the GOP for the 1994 congressional elections, leading the Republican takeover of the House and Senate in 1994.

Conclusion

The Republican and Democratic coalitions are now both in a state of flux, driven by the recognition that the United States is subject to terrorist assault and by the ongoing violence in the Middle East. Both the terrorist threat and the wars in Afghanistan and Iraq worked initially to the advantage of the Republican Party and played to the GOP edge on matters of national defense and the use of force, but it is not at all clear what the long-term partisan consequences will be, much less where the war on terror and the U.S. involvement overseas will lead. These factors are virtually certain to radically affect what has been the modest, but consistent, conservative national tilt of American politics during the past four decades and to reformulate the issues of domestic social and cultural upheaval, which have recently played such a decisive role in American politics.

PART TWO

New Democrats

CHAPTER THREE

Incomplete Victory: The Rise of the New Democrats

William A. Galston

Introduction: The Dynamics of Party Change

My task in this essay is to explain the rise and significance of the New Democratic movement within the Democratic Party. Because this rise is an instance of a more general phenomenon—party change—I begin with some broad reflections on the dynamics of party change in the United States.

In one of their few notable failures of insight, the drafters of the U.S. Constitution did not foresee that the electoral system they constructed created incentives for the formation of political parties and pressures to consolidate factions into a small number of major aggregations. Through most of the past two centuries, American politics has been dominated by competition between two principal parties—for the past century and a half, between the same two parties. With but a few exceptions (the collapse of the Federalists and Whigs, the rise of the Republicans), political change has taken place through transformations within established parties.

As one reflects on the history of intraparty change in the United States, four sources emerge as key. The first is the simple logic of party competition. In many respects, our political system is much closer to winner-take-all than are most parliamentary systems. Members of political parties have strong incentives, therefore, to settle for nothing less than victory. A string of defeats at the hands of the opposition will generate pressures for change. For example, Dwight Eisenhower's modern Republicanism reflected the recognition that the New Deal had become a permanent feature of American politics and that continued opposition to it would consign Republicans to irrelevance. Another source of competitive pressure is the rise of third parties that threaten to erode existing majorities or to thwart the formation of new ones. Republicans dealt far more successfully with the 1968 insurgency of George Wallace than did Democrats, whereas Democrats dealt more successfully with Ross Perot's challenge in 1992. Both cases, however, resulted in multiple victories in presidential contests.

Fundamental shifts in the economy and society constitute a second principal source of party change. The post–Civil War shift from agriculture and individual entrepreneurship to large corporations and mass production created stresses and opportunities on which the Republican Party was able to capitalize, culminating in the realigning election of 1896. Demographic shifts, whether generated externally through immigration or internally through large birth cohorts, create political opportunities—namely, substantial pools of potential new voters with distinctive concerns.

A third source of change takes the form of shocks, or events that produce a rupture with the past and to which political parties are compelled to respond. Two classic examples are the Great Depression, which opened the door to an enlarged and restructured national government, and Pearl Harbor, which ended the debate between isolationists and internationalists that had dominated the interwar period. By taking the side of big government at home and robust engagement abroad, Democrats captured the political high ground and held it for two generations. (The current Bush administration is doing everything it can to make the case that September 11 represents another such transformative external shock.) Sometimes these reorienting shocks originate within the political system itself. During the past fifty years, for example, Supreme Court decisions on school integration, school prayer, and abortion have forced both parties to respond. It would not have been easy for political observers in 1954 to predict that Democrats would become the party of civil rights, reproductive choice, and strict separation between church and state. But so it proved, and in the process, the dynamics of party competition were transformed.

What I call "redefining ideas" constitute the fourth and final source of party change. Ideas enter the political system through two routes, which might be stylized as bottom-up and top-down. Throughout the twentieth century, popularly based social movements conveyed ideas to political parties. Civil rights, women's rights, prohibition, and environmentalism are instances drawn from a very long list. In other cases, however, scholars and policy activists without a popular base can directly influence party elites. Herbert Croly's *The Promise of American Life* influenced two generations of progressive leaders. Keynesian economics, which reconfigured the Democratic Party, and supply-side economics, which did the same for Republicans, were, in the main, transactions between elites that generated, rather than were generated by, popular movements.

Before turning to a detailed examination of the rise of the New Democrats, let me use the fourfold template of party change I have sketched above to characterize, in broad strokes, the forces that fueled the movement. There can be no doubt, to begin, that interparty competition was a major motivation. The New Democratic movement began to take shape in the immediate wake of Walter Mondale's defeat. Between 1968 and 1984, Democrats lost four of five presidential elections, two by historic landslides. And Michael Dukakis's 1988 loss to George H. W. Bush propelled New Democrats into a far more aggressive stance within their party.

Socioeconomic change played a smaller, but still perceptible, role. During the early 1980s, the emergence of a technology-based postindustrial and service economy led some Democrats to wonder whether New Deal policies and arrangements, rooted as they were in mass industrial production, would serve either the country or the party well in the late twentieth century.

Transformative shocks played almost no role in the rise of the New Democrats. In contrast to many other episodes of party change, it is hard to point to a pivotal event in the economy, in the international arena, or even in the judicial system. To be sure, the fall of the Berlin Wall and the collapse of communism were momentous, but they had a remarkably small impact on the substance of New Democrats' policy development, and not much more on their political fortunes—or so I shall argue.

Finally, New Democrats worked, with some success, to use redefining ideas as a source of political change. Perhaps fatefully, however, these ideas entered the political system from the top rather than the bottom. Unlike the Goldwater-Reagan transformation of the Republican Party, New Democrats did not rely on, and for some time did little to create, a grassroots movement of committed activists. As a result, Bill Clinton, the quintessential New Democratic standard-bearer, prevailed in 1992 on the strength of ideas that enjoyed wider acceptance among the American people as a whole than they did within his own party. The contrast between the fractious executive-legislative relations during the first two years of Clinton's presidency and the disciplined interbranch cooperation during the first two years of George W. Bush's is stark.

The Historical Context: Party Change, 1961–1980

My thesis in this section is that profound changes within both political parties, from the inauguration of John F. Kennedy to the election of Ronald Reagan, laid the political predicate for the emergence of the New Democratic movement. Let me begin with the Democrats.

Economics

Kennedy took office determined to accelerate economic growth after the two recessions in Eisenhower's second term, and he was confident that growth would promote the general welfare. After all, he remarked, "A rising tide lifts all boats." At the same time, his encounter with poverty during the West Virginia primary had shocked and moved him. One of his earliest legislative proposals was the Area Redevelopment Act, targeted on Appalachia. By emphasizing measures such as the War on Poverty, Lyndon Johnson more fully associated Democrats with the redistributive dimension of economic policy. Under the control of George McGovern's forces, the 1972 Democratic convention drafted the most aggressively redistributionist platform in the party's recent history. For his part, Jimmy Carter came close to challenging the very desirability of growth by associating his administration with stringent energy conservation and the "limits to growth" thesis popularized by the Club of Rome. Meanwhile, soaring inflation weakened public confidence in Carter's stewardship of the economy. By the election of 1980, the link between the Democratic Party and economic growth had frayed.

Defense and Foreign Policy

During the 1960 election, John Kennedy ran to Nixon's right on defense and foreign policy, charging that the Eisenhower administration had failed to prosecute the cold war with vigor and had allowed a missile gap to develop with the Soviet Union. His cold war liberalism combined support for international institutions and law with a willingness to use force on behalf of American interests and values. The Vietnam War shattered this consensus by driving a wedge between international engagement and the deployment of power. The 1972 Democratic platform called not only for unilateral U.S. withdrawal from Vietnam but also for troop cuts in Europe, steep reductions in military expenditures, and an end to the draft. Although more moderate in tone and substance, the 1976 Democratic platform advocated cutting weapons systems, reducing reliance on military force as an instrument of foreign policy, and emphasizing the pursuit of human rights rather than the traditional concerns of realpolitik. The Carter administration's inability to resolve its internal disputes about relations with the Soviets, as well as its ambivalence about the use of force, contributed to a series of overseas reverses and raised public doubts about the Democratic Party's stewardship of defense and foreign policy.

Social and Cultural Issues

During the 1960s and 1970s, the Democratic Party's orientation on social and cultural issues underwent a profound transformation. The party moved from ambivalence and division to a wholehearted embrace of civil rights for African Americans. It moved from a male-dominated organization in which women's rights and concerns were given short shrift to the endorsement of legalized abortion and the Equal Rights Amendment. The party's views on crime and criminal justice reflected a shift away from punishment and toward sociological explanations ("root causes") and alternatives to incarceration. Once firmly grounded in the cultural mainstream, the party opened itself to the counterculture, most conspicuously at its 1972 convention, at which the platform endorsed the "right to be different." With increasing fervor, Democrats embraced a legalistically strict separation of church and state, creating at least the perception of a basically secularist orientation.

Stance Toward Government

At the core of the New Deal outlook was a deep faith in government, as the local of public-spirited action and as the most effective vehicle for accomplishing a range of collective tasks. Despite some tonal novelties, the Kennedy administration shared that faith. By the Carter administration, however, that faith had mutated into something close to its opposite. Under the impact of Vietnam and Watergate, trust in the essential integrity of government had been replaced by the presumption of self-serving venality and dishonesty. Substantial portions of the party had shifted from confidence in government as the engine of social and economic reform to deep ambivalence. In his 1978 State of the Union address, Jimmy Carter said:

> Government cannot solve our problems. It cannot set our goals. It cannot define our vision. Government cannot eliminate poverty or provide a bountiful economy or reduce inflation, or save our cities, or cure illiteracy, or provide energy. And government cannot mandate goodness. . . . Those of us who govern can sometimes inspire. And we can identify needs and marshal resources. But we simply cannot be the managers of everything and everybody.

On one level, of course, President Carter had done nothing more than state obvious truths about the relation between government and the people. On another level, however, his declaration amounted to a repudiation of the New Deal's vision of governance. Certainly, it was so understood by a substantial portion of his own party, helping to fuel Edward Kennedy's insurgency against him.

The Democratic Party

Between 1961 and 1980, the Democratic Party had been transformed, institutionally and politically. As a result of the post-1968 changes in party rules, its governance structure shifted away from mediating institutions, such as state and local parties, and toward more direct forms of participation; away from delegate selection through closed, hierarchical party structures and toward reliance on primaries and caucuses. At the same time, power within the party began to shift away from relatively broadly based organizations, such as the AFL-CIO, and toward narrower advocacy groups organized around ethnicity, gender, or specific issue concerns. Reflecting this emerging group orientation, the party endorsed equal representation of men and women on all convention committees and called upon state parties to take "affirmative steps" to provide representation to women, minorities, and young people in "reasonable relationship" to their percentage of each state's population.[1]

Finally, the political base of the Democratic Party was changing. As late as 1960, the Republican presidential nominee was able to garner one-third of the African American vote. By 1980, African American support for Democrats was nearly unanimous. At the same time and reflecting broader changes in the economy, middle-class professionals were providing an increasing share of the party's total support. (It was the differences of outlook and interests between these professionals and the industrial working class that fueled the 1984 primary contest between Gary Hart and Walter Mondale.) Within organized labor itself, industrial unions, which tended to be white, male, and strongly anticommunist, were in decline, whereas public-sector unions, which tended to be more diverse, female, and dovish, were gaining members and élan. Disaffected on racial, cultural, and religious issues, white Southern Protestants deserted the party in droves, shifting the Democratic center of gravity toward the Northern tier and the two coasts.

In key respects, the tale of Democratic Party transformation is one hand clapping because the changes in the Republican Party were equally profound (and in some respects symmetrical). Although Eisenhower split with Robert Taft by accepting the legacy of the New Deal, he agreed with Taft about the importance of government frugality and balanced budgets. Although the 1964 Goldwater insurgency did not cause an immediate takeover of the Republican Party, it did energize a grassroots conservative movement that worked fervently for a smaller, less intrusive government. After a detour through Nixon's

---

1. Jules Witcover, *Party of the People: A History of the Democrats* (New York: Random House, 2003), 574.

embrace of Keynesian fiscal policy and wage and price controls, by the end of the 1970s, Republicans had become the party of tax cuts and supply-side economics. In foreign policy, the party shifted from détente to a confrontation with communism framed in quasi-Wilsonian terms. The entrance of large numbers of evangelicals and social conservatives moved the party toward the advocacy of "traditional values." As a result, the Republican political base shifted away from the Northeast, and to some extent from the Midwest, and toward the Sunbelt.

It is easy to forget how recently the Republican Party that we now take for granted came into being. A glance at the party's 1972 platform is instructive. The opening section lays out a systematic effort to define and seize the political center, summarized in the following passage:

> This year the choice is between moderate goals historically sought by both major parties and far-out goals of the far left. The contest is not between the two great parties Americans have known in previous years. For in this year 1972 the national Democratic Party has been seized by a radical clique which scorns our nation's past and would blight her future.

In foreign policy, the document highlighted Nixon's trip to China, improved cooperation with the Soviet Union (including arms control treaties), and dozens of new international agreements. In addition to wage and price controls, the economic section of the platform featured initiatives, such as tax reform tilted toward the middle class and the poor, as well as a vigorous antitrust policy. The domestic policy section combined conservative positions on a handful of "backlash" issues (busing, welfare, crime, and drugs) with liberal stances on virtually everything else, including (among hundreds of items) affordable medical insurance, community mental health centers, increased spending for education and children's programs, and major urban mass transit legislation. The platform pointed with pride to the administration's pathbreaking environmental record, including the creation of new executive branch agencies and the enactment of sweeping legislation addressing nearly every key environmental problem. The section on civil rights endorsed affirmative action, stepped-up federal enforcement of equal employment opportunity, voting representation in Congress for the District of Columbia, legislation and a constitutional amendment to lower the voting age, and ratification of the Equal Rights Amendment.

Notably, the 1972 Republican platform said nothing whatever about abortion. For that matter, neither did the Democratic platform. The abortion issue offers a case study of how an exogenous shock (in this instance, the *Roe v. Wade* decision) can, over time, force both parties to respond and change. The result was a symmetrical widening of the breach between the parties on what proved to be a defining issue.

In 1976, the Democrats said of abortion only that

> We fully recognize the religious and ethical nature of the concerns which many Americans have on the subject of abortion. We feel, however, that it is undesirable to attempt to amend the U.S. Constitutions to overturn the Supreme Court decision in this area.

By 1980, while adopting roughly the same legal and policy stance, the Democrats' language was more supportive of the pro-choice position:

> We fully recognize the religious and ethical concerns which many Americans have about abortion. We also recognize the belief of many Americans that a woman has a right to choose whether and when to have a child. The Democratic party supports the 1973 Supreme Court decision as the law of the land and opposes any constitutional amendment to restrict or overturn that decision.

By 1984, the party abandoned any verbal recognition of the concerns of abortion opponents and recast the issue in moral terms:

> The Democratic party recognizes reproductive freedom as a fun-

damental human right. We therefore oppose government interference in the reproductive freedom of Americans, especially government interference which denies poor Americans their right to privacy by funding or advocating one or a limited number of reproductive choices only.

A parallel evolution occurred within the Republican Party. Although both the 1976 and 1980 platforms endorsed a constitutional amendment to reverse *Roe*, each acknowledged, at length, the diversity of legitimate views within the party. For example, the 1976 discussion began by declaring:

> The question of abortion is one of the most difficult and controversial of our time. It is undoubtedly a moral and personal issue but it also involves complex questions relating to medical science and criminal justice. There are those in our Party who favor complete support for the Supreme Court decision which permits abortion on demand. There are others who share sincere convictions that the Supreme Court's decision must be changed by a constitutional amendment prohibiting all abortions. Others have yet to take a position, or they have assumed a stance somewhere in between polar positions.

It was not until 1984 that the Republican Party, mirror-imaging the Democrats, expunged all reference to legitimate diversity within the party and recast the issue as a fundamental moral conflict about which compromise was unthinkable:

> The unborn child has a fundamental individual right to life which cannot be infringed. We therefore reaffirm our support for a human life amendment to the Constitution, and we endorse legislation to make clear that the Fourteenth Amendment's protections apply to unborn children. We oppose the use of public revenues for abortion and will eliminate funding for organizations which advocate or support abortions.

Similar stories could be told in several other areas. I would hazard the following generalization: the stark cultural cleavages we now take for granted as a defining (and, in many ways, disfiguring) feature of American politics represent choices that the parties made over time in response to external events. Whether these issues could have played out differently—that is, whether they could have become matters of argument within parties rather than warfare between them—is one of the imponderables of our recent political history.

Defeat and Dismay: The Rise of the New Democrats

The vicissitudes of the Democratic Party in the two decades between the election of John F. Kennedy and the defeat of Jimmy Carter sparked two waves of intraparty debate. Although the focus of this essay is on the second of these waves, it is useful to begin by sketching the first.

The 1972 Democratic convention deeply traumatized key elements of the liberal coalition. "Cold war liberals," including many prominent northeastern intellectuals, had long supported a muscular anticommunist democratic internationalism, an activist state in economic and social policy, and a moderate form of moral traditionalism. In all these respects, cold war liberals were comfortable with organized labor as led by George Meany and Lane Kirkland. Most of these liberals had backed Lyndon Johnson's Great Society programs, including the War on Poverty. The setbacks these programs encountered, and the unexpected consequences they engendered, led many liberals to question their faith in the power of activist government to remake society. These doubts, which helped catalyze the founding of an influential new journal (*The Public Interest*), constituted one of the key building blocks of what came to be known as neoconservatism.

These liberals were also critical of the counterculture. They believed in sobriety, moderation, self-restraint, respect for authority, and the rule of law—indeed, the panoply of bourgeois virtues. They rejected the counterculture's critique of these virtues, and they could not stomach the romantic antinomianism, much in evidence on the floor of the 1972 convention, with which the counterculture sought to replace them.

More than any other factor, however, it was foreign policy concerns that sparked the rise of neoconservatism. As we have seen, the 1972 Democratic Party platform turned its back on a quarter-century of liberal anticommunism. In an effort to turn back the tide, cold war liberals clustered around the 1976 primary campaign of the quintessential liberal anticommunist, Senator Henry "Scoop" Jackson. After Jackson's campaign failed, many invested their hopes in Jimmy Carter, who, although unconventional and virtually unclassifiable, was at least a Southerner and former naval officer who might have been expected to resist the McGovernist thrust in foreign policy. Carter's failure to do so until he was surprised by the Soviet invasion of Afghanistan led many cold war liberals to support the candidacy of Ronald Reagan. By the early 1980s, neoconservatism was a spent force within the Democratic Party, although some cold war liberals remained within the party and banded together in organizations such as the Coalition for a Democratic Majority, conducting an often lonely struggle to restore a lost consensus.

The neoconservative exodus from the Democratic Party virtually coincided with the first stirrings of the New Democrat movement. As we will see, at the outset, New Democrats were less concerned with ideology than were the neoconservatives and more concerned about the imperative of regaining a national majority. Although sharing neoconservatives' reservations about a McGovernist foreign policy, they cared more about domestic policy. Having come to political maturity after the Great Society, they were less seared by the alleged failure of activist government, less committed to retrenchment, and more committed to reform. While offering a new moral basis for public policy, they did not feel besieged by the counterculture, which, in any event, had been watered down and domesticated. Finally, although offering a robust defense of what they termed "democratic capitalism," New Democrats were not as close to organized labor as many neoconservatives had been. Indeed, New Democrats came to see unions as often creating narrowly self-interested obstacles to forward-looking policies and necessary reforms.

Walter Mondale's ill-fated presidential campaign brought discontent within the Democratic Party to a boil and helped spark the New Democratic movement. (Full disclosure: I served as Mondale's issues director throughout the campaign.) At the outset, Mondale hoped to run as the unifier of the Democratic Party, bridging its post-Vietnam internal divisions. But in response to the demands of the primary process and Gary Hart's surprisingly strong challenge, Mondale defined himself in ways that exacerbated fissures within the party over economic, foreign policy, and cultural issues.

This process continued throughout the general election. Mondale responded to President Reagan's supply-side budget deficits by running as a fiscal conservative, proposing spending restraints and a tax increase to restore fiscal discipline. He responded to Reagan's aggressive defense and foreign policies by emphasizing cooperation with our allies and arms negotiations with the Soviets. He countered Reagan's embrace of conservative Protestant evangelicals by insisting on strict separation between church and state.

During the campaign, three overlapping but distinct sources of intraparty discontent and dissent emerged: Southern Democrats, who were deeply troubled by the party's growing weakness in their region, a weakness that threatened statewide Democratic officeholders as well as members of Congress; the staunchly anti-Soviet followers of Scoop Jackson, who couldn't bring themselves to follow the neoconservatives into the Republican Party; and the so-called "Atari Democrats," who believed that the shift from an industrial to a high-tech economy required new policies and institutional arrangements, including the diminution of the influence of organized labor within the Democratic Party. The concerns of these groups overlapped in complex ways. Hailing from a region with weak unions (and in many cases weak right-to-work laws), Southerners tended to sympathize with the Atari

Democrats' skepticism about the relevance of New Deal–style labor organizations. A rising generation of progressive Southern governors understood that only new kinds of economic opportunities and increased investment in human capital could relieve their states' historic underdevelopment. Despite their differences with organized labor, however, the Southerners were comfortable with the union-based Scoop Jackson Democrats' support for robust defense and foreign policies. And being forced to forge majorities in a region known for traditional cultural and social views, they were sensitive to the need to moderate the party's post-1972 tilt to the Left on issues such as welfare, crime, and the role of religion in public life.

The institutional flagship of the New Democratic movement, the Democratic Leadership Council, opened for business in February 1985. Its early years, ably chronicled in Kenneth Baer's *Reinventing Democrats*, were marked by unsuccessful efforts to place the traditional party machinery and electoral rules in the service of more moderate voices within the party. As the 1988 election approached, the DLC helped engineer "Super Tuesday" (March 8, 1988), when Democrats in twenty mostly Southern states were to go to the polls. The hope was that the more moderate Southern voters would dilute the influence of Iowa and New Hampshire, forcing candidates toward the center and giving credible moderates a better chance of prevailing.

Events did not justify these hopes. To be sure, the New Democrats' young champion, Albert Gore Jr., prevailed in four Southern states. But Jesse Jackson won five, while the eventual nominee, Michael Dukakis, carried off the biggest prizes—Florida and Texas. Super Tuesday demonstrated that Reagan had reconfigured Southern politics by drawing conservative Democrats into the Republican Party, leaving Southern Democrats with a coalition increasingly dominated by white liberals and African Americans. (This was especially the case during the primaries, which typically attract the more committed voters.) Although the DLC's base among Southern-elected officials remained formidable, it became clear that a political strategy focused on the South would no longer suffice to rebuild a national majority.

Michael Dukakis's defeat in 1988 had a greater impact on the Democratic Party than did Walter Mondale's loss four years earlier. After all, Mondale had lost to one of the greatest political communicators of the twentieth century, during a year in which the economy expanded robustly, the country was at peace, and the people could be persuaded that it was indeed "Morning in America." By mid-1984, few really expected Mondale to win; the question was whether his defeat would be respectable or (as it turned out) catastrophic. In contrast, by mid-1988, Dukakis had surged to a 17-point margin over George H. W. Bush. He was running as an able economic manager, the architect of the "Massachusetts miracle." The issue, he declared, was competence, not ideology. Nonetheless, the Bush campaign succeeded in portraying Dukakis as a liberal who was untested in defense and foreign policy while being out of touch with the social and cultural concerns of mainstream Americans. By September, Bush was in the lead.

In November, Dukakis lost, not only white Southerners but also Catholics, moderates, independents, and voters in the heart of the middle class. His defeat threw the Democratic Party into near crisis. According to traditional liberals close to organized labor, Dukakis lost because he had muted his differences with Republicans and had failed to offer voters a clear choice—there was nothing wrong with liberalism that full-throated advocacy couldn't cure. The DLC drew the opposite conclusion: Dukakis's defeat proved that contemporary liberalism, an amalgam of New Deal, Great Society, and McGovernite propositions and programs, had lost credibility and was no longer politically viable. The issue was ideology, not competence, but the ideology of the past could not serve as an effective counterweight to Reaganism. Nothing less than a new approach would do.

Having drawn this conclusion, the DLC abandoned its initial effort to play a meliorist, nonconfrontational game within the party structure and went into open opposition. A key move was the founding of its own think tank, the Progressive Policy Institute (PPI), with the express aim of creating a new Democratic agenda and governing philosophy. In 1989, the DLC published a political and ideological manifesto, "The Politics of Evasion." (More full disclosure: I was its coauthor, along with Elaine Kamarck.) The manifesto argued that Democrats had lost ground since the 1970s because the American people had come to see the party as inattentive to their economic interests, indifferent to their cultural concerns, and ineffective in defense of the country's interests abroad. To prevail, the next Democratic nominee would have to present himself as a wise steward of the people's resources, sympathetic to the cultural mainstream, and trustworthy as commander in chief. To nominate such a candidate, the party would have to set aside three entrenched myths: that it could forge a majority by mobilizing the few groups whose loyalty it still commanded; that it could win by nominating a more fervent liberal; and that it could continue to control the Congress despite repeated defeats at the presidential level. The manifesto buttressed these arguments with electoral, demographic, and survey data. It became the template for the thematic and policy development that largely occupied the DLC and PPI between 1989 and 1992.

The authors of the new progressive agenda that was worked out during those years understood it as an ensemble of innovative means to traditional progressive ends. On the domestic front, the dominant goal was to create an inclusive society unified around the principle of "equal opportunity for all, special privileges for none." In foreign policy, the guiding purpose was to foster, to the extent prudence permits, the worldwide spread of democracy. Although this new progressive agenda called for, and required, a reformed but activist state, it broke with the statist progressivism of the early twentieth century by arguing that a vigorous civil society and shared norms were also needed to achieve historic progressive ends.

However, the new progressive agenda did not simply ratify the aims of contemporary liberalism. Indeed, it rested on three themes, each of which contrasted with contemporary liberalism as well as Reagan conservatism. *Equal opportunity* stood in opposition both to guarantees of equal outcomes and to pure Darwinian competition. Achieving equal opportunity required vigorous, well-targeted public policies, but it was up to individuals to take advantage of the opportunities made available to them. *Reciprocal responsibility* stood in opposition both to the philosophy of entitlement (getting without giving) and to pure individualism (you're on your own). Well-crafted public policies would bring together contributions and rewards. Finally, *community* stood in opposition both to rights-based individualism (the dominant ethos of modern liberalism) and to the cultural conservative ethos of promoting moral behavior through state coercion. The progressive ethic of community implied that as citizens we're all in this together and that one of the purposes of politics is to locate, and build upon, moral sentiments that we can freely share.

New Democrats framed these themes with a historical analogy. At the end of the nineteenth century, the transition from an agricultural to an industrial economy drove profound changes in American society and made necessary a new public philosophy and new approaches to economics, culture, political institutions, and foreign relations. The progressives' response to these challenges, set forth in works such as Herbert Croly's *The Promise of American Life*, found early champions in political leaders such as Theodore Roosevelt and Hiram Johnson and reached full flower in FDR's New Deal. At the end of the twentieth century, the United States was undergoing an equivalent transition, from an industrial to a postindustrial economy, with equally profound consequences for our society and politics. The challenge for New Democrats was to understand the practical implications of these changes and to express them in innovative public policies.

Reflecting on these changes, New Democrats drew a number of conclusions that guided policy development. First, economic transition implied changes in the structure of opportunity. Individuals' economic prospects were likely to depend less on collective arrangements and more on their own individual training and skills. Second, changes in the basis of income and wealth implied shifts in the electorate. As the middle class came to be dominated by professionals and "knowledge workers," its outlook would change as well: the new middle class was likely to be less concerned with guaranteed security and more interested in opportunity, choice, and rewards commensurate with their contributions. Third, markets would play a more central role in the new economy than in the old industrial economy, and the playing field would tilt against both industrial-era oligopolies and increasingly sclerotic public bureaucracies. This implied, in turn, the need for a reformed government that made more effective use of choice, market mechanisms, and new information technology. These themes and broad propositions drove detailed policy developments, of which I can present only the highlights.

To overcome Reagan-era budget deficits and to set the stage for sustained economic growth, the New Democrats' economic policy began with fiscal discipline, including cutting programs and closing corporate tax loopholes. Forward-looking features of economic policy included a focus on innovation and entrepreneurship, a new emphasis on education and training, and a range of mechanisms (which came to be known collectively as "democratic capitalism") for ensuring that workers in the new economy were able to obtain a fair share of its rewards. To address the problems of the working poor, New Democrats advocated a dramatic expansion of the Earned Income Tax Credit (EITC) rather than the industrial-era minimum wage. In another break with policies advocated by organized labor, New Democrats endorsed free trade treaties and steadily increasing global openness as the core of international economics.

In domestic policy, New Democrats developed policies based on three principles: using market mechanisms for progressive purposes, aligning programs with mainstream values, and reinforcing an ethic of reciprocity. Examples of the first included market-based health insurance and environmental regulation; of the second, welfare reform, 100,000 new police in local communities, and policies to shore up the two-parent family; and of the third, a new program of national and community service that would provide full-time volunteers with substantial postservice benefits to fund education and training.

In foreign policy, finally, New Democrats developed policies that put our diplomacy and armed forces in the service not only of our interests but also of our ideals. The end of the cold war did not mean the end of danger, but it did require new equipment, weapons systems, and training consistent with the changing mission of the U.S. military. The focus was not on cuts, as many liberals advocated, but rather on investments in reform. Overall, the emphasis was on "democratic internationalism"—comprehensive engagement abroad to promote democratization and deeper cooperation among democratic nations.

Bill Clinton's emergence as the New Democratic standard-bearer is an oft-told tale that I will not repeat here. Suffice it to say that he combined an intellectual mastery of policy detail with an intuitive flair for framing arguments to appeal to diverse constituencies, including traditional liberals. During the 1992 campaign, Ross Perot's surprising rise reflected, and gave new momentum to, concerns about the budget deficit, creating a political predicate for New Democratic fiscal restraint. At the same time, the waning of the cold war and rapid end to the first Gulf War reduced the salience of defense and foreign policy concerns, which were not Clinton's strong suit. The real pivot turned out to be values-laden domestic policy issues. Clinton convinced a key segment of the electorate that he was serious about breaking with Democrats' previous approaches to welfare and crime. The campaign's key TV spot, featured in swing states in the crucial two weeks before election day, went as follows:

They're a new generation of Democrats, Bill Clinton and Al Gore. And they don't think the way the Old Democratic Party did. They've called for an end to welfare as we know it, so welfare can be a second chance, not a way of life. They've sent a strong signal to criminals by supporting the death penalty. And they've rejected the old tax-and-spend policies.[2]

Bill Clinton's Presidency and the Future of the New Democratic Movement

Many analysts have observed that the first two years of the Clinton administration were a mixed bag for New Democrats and a disaster for the Democratic Party. I do not dissent from either of these judgments. Because the latter is so obviously true, let me focus on the former.

In economic policy, despite pitched battles within the White House and the party, Clinton stuck to New Democratic guns far more that most predicted. Early on, he rejected traditional fiscal stimulus in favor of restraint and deficit reduction. With a characteristic mix of persuasive public advocacy and one-on-one politics, he managed to move his controversial free trade agenda forward, getting both the North American Free Trade Agreement (NAFTA) and the latest round of General Agreement on Tariffs and Trade (GATT) through the Congress, over staunch Democratic opposition.

Domestic policy presented a very different picture. In a shoot-out between traditional liberals and New Democrats, the president gave priority to health care over welfare reform, with disastrous results. Although his crime bill did include substantial federal support for more police on the streets in local communities, the debate in Congress highlighted the issue of gun control, a significant negative for many Southern and rural Democratic members. Other high-profile social issues included the unfortunate controversy over gays in the

2. Quoted in Witcover, *Party of the People*, 663.

military, executive orders that adopted an uncompromising position on abortion, and a racial discussion dominated by the failed nomination of Lani Guinier as Assistant Attorney General for Civil Rights.

In the area of governance and citizenship, things went better. Under the leadership of Vice President Gore, government reform and reinvention moved forward on a broad front. Presidential leadership was also key to early passage of legislation restructuring and expanding opportunities for national and community service, though not as much as New Democrats had hoped.

Defense and foreign policy were far less successful, in part because Clinton's interests lay elsewhere during the early years and also because senior administration leaders proved unable to forge a hard-edged consensus or, in some instances, even to manage their own agencies effectively. The results were a muddle in the Balkans, an embarrassing flip-flop on trade with China, and a fiasco in Somalia, the reverberations of which extended far beyond the borders of that unfortunate country. Had these reverses not coincided with a period of low public concerns about foreign affairs, the political consequences might well have been quite serious.

In sum, then, the first two years of the Clinton presidency offered two clear wins for the New Democrats, one win for traditional liberals, and one irrelevant draw. The liberal victory occurred in domestic social policy, which was highly visible, intensely controversial, and largely unsuccessful. The president's New Democratic economic policies were slow to show gains, while the governance agenda had much less political salience. As a result, Clinton's profile was largely defined and judged in traditional liberal, rather than reformist New Democratic, terms. The result was a rout in the 1994 elections, with Democrats losing control of both houses of Congress for the first time in more than forty years.

In several respects, Clinton fared better with the Republican-dominated Congress during his second two years. He managed to resist ill-judged and draconian budget cuts while laying the foundation for an eventual bipartisan balanced budget deal. After blocking welfare bills that he regarded as unbalanced, he was able to redeem his campaign pledge to "end welfare as we know it." (His decision to sign the legislation highlighted continuing disputes between liberals and New Democrats and sparked several resignations from his administration.) As his economic policies took hold and growth shifted into a higher gear, public sentiment turned steadily in his direction and he was able to win a comfortable victory over Bob Dole in the 1996 presidential election.

From a New Democratic perspective, however, the victory came at a price. Following the 1994 defeat, Clinton turned to a controversial operative, Dick Morris, as his principal political advisor. Morris advocated and helped execute a strategy of what he called "triangulation," designed to lift the president above, and position him apart from, both political parties. The placement of a series of New Democratic proposals within this political frame helped tarnish the movement's agenda with the brush of political opportunism. This, in turn, fed the (mistaken) view that Clinton's acceptance of a balanced budget and welfare reform were the products of calculation rather than principle.

As a result, many more Left-leaning Democrats began characterizing the New Democratic agenda as not only wrongheaded but also deeply cynical. In the aftermath of Clinton's budget deal with the Republicans in the summer of 1997, House minority leader Richard Gephardt declared that the agreement represented not only "a deficit of fairness, a deficit of tax justice, and . . . a deficit of dollars" but also a "deficit of principle." In a December 1997 speech regarded as laying the foundation for an eventual presidential candidacy, Gephardt broadened his critique:

> New Democrats . . . [are those] who set their compass only off the direction of others—who talk about the political center, but fail to understand that if it is only defined by others, it lacks core values.

And who too often market a political strategy masquerading as policy.[3]

The final years of the Clinton administration represent a huge missed opportunity. Had it not been for the atmosphere of scandal and political conflict, exacerbating the already high level of partisan rancor, it might have been possible to take advantage of prosperity and the mounting budget surplus to address some long-deferred challenges and to place troubled entitlement programs on a sounder basis for the future. Instead, the administration made sporadic proposals (often in the annual State of the Union speeches) and then resorted to holding actions designed to ward off Republican tax cuts.

One especially unfortunate result of the lingering scandal was that the party's 2000 presidential nominee, Vice President Gore, felt compelled to distance himself from the president whom he had served so loyally and ably. In the process of effecting this separation, he deemphasized the administration's very real achievements, many of which rested on New Democratic foundations, and resorted to a generic populist message that blurred the party's future.

Conclusion: The New Democratic
Movement and the Future of the Party

As I draft this essay, shortly after the end of the 2004 primary season, the Democratic Party's future is still in doubt. Although deeply controversial within the party, the DLC's early intervention against Howard Dean (as a return to McGovernism) helped lay the foundation for his defeat. On the other hand, the only candidate to hew faithfully to the New Democratic creed, Joe Lieberman, failed to gain any traction whatever. Nor, interestingly, did the candidate backed by most of organized labor fare well. Dick Gephardt did miserably in Iowa, where industrial unions remain influential, and soon left the race. The

3. Quoted in Witcover, *Party of the People*, 683.

winning candidate made himself generally acceptable to all the party's principal factions while clearly articulating the principles of none. In an atmosphere polarized by the policies of the Bush administration and rendered desperate by Republican control of all branches of government, Democrats were less interested than in years past in partisan wrangling and more concerned about maximizing their chances of victory.

Some divisive issues from the past are now off the table. Crime and welfare are not the burning controversies they were a decade ago. For better or worse, the party no longer debates abortion or affirmative action. And most party leaders have now accepted, some more grudgingly than others, the basic outlines of the Clinton formula for fiscal discipline.

Differences remain, of course. Trade emerged as the most divisive economic issue of the primary campaign, with the New Democrat position on the defensive. Even John Kerry, a longtime free trader, felt compelled to make protectionist noises, while John Edwards (a fresh face and able campaigner who enjoyed significant support among New Democrats) sounded like a senator from a state with a dying textile industry. On the foreign policy front, the war in Iraq reopened some of the party's Vietnam-era wounds. Here again, the New Democratic position came under pressure: Two of the three senators in the race who had voted for the fall 2002 resolution authorizing President Bush to take action ended up opposing the $87 billion supplemental appropriation for troop support and Iraqi reconstruction; they became the Democratic Party's 2004 presidential and vice-presidential nominees. One cannot help suspecting that they would have supported the appropriation absent the rigors of the primary campaign.[4]

4. Senator Joseph Biden, a close adviser to Senator Kerry, has been quoted as saying that Kerry's decision not to support the $87 billion appropriation was "tactical," an effort to "prove to Dean's guys [that] I'm not a warmonger." See Philip Gourevitch, "Damage Control," *New Yorker*, 26 July 2004: 55.

Toward the beginning of this essay, I remarked that Bill Clinton won the presidency in 1992 on the basis of New Democratic ideas that enjoyed significant support in the country as a whole, but less support within his own party. Today, nearly twelve years later, less has changed than might have been expected. Bill Clinton failed to institutionalize his political success. Despite the DLC's energetic efforts, New Democrats have yet to become a real grassroots movement. They do constitute a growing network of state and local elected officials, but they are still a minority. New Democrats continue to supply the bulk of fresh proposals for the party, but they often win the battle of ideas only to lose the war of votes.

The 2004 Democratic Party convention illustrated the problem. While the delegates obediently ratified the party's platform and cheered its nominees, surveys showed that they stood well to the left of the platform and the nominees' muscular acceptance speeches on domestic and foreign policy as well as on social issues. The party that John Kerry and John Edwards lead into battle is temporarily united, not around ideas but rather around its burning desire to remove George W. Bush from the presidency.

If the Kerry/Edwards ticket prevails, we can expect early battles between traditional liberals and New Democrats. The presidential transition might well witness a replay of the November 1992–January 1993 struggle within the nascent Clinton administration between the advocates of increased domestic spending and the proponents of fiscal restraint. For example, the president-elect might have to make a choice between an immediate push for his massive health care proposal and his pledge to cut the deficit by half within four years.

On the other hand, if the Kerry/Edwards ticket goes down to defeat, the usual cycle of intraparty recriminations will resume as the pent-up energy and resentment of traditional liberals who held their peace in the name of victory bursts forth. The candidacy of Howard Dean showed where the hearts of the party's grassroots activists really lie, and it is difficult to believe that they would not find champions of their cause with presidential ambitions.

In short, while some of the issues that have divided traditional liberals and new Democrats since the 1980s have faded, others remain salient and the war in Iraq has created passionate new cleavages. Whether the 2004 ticket wins or loses, it is safe to predict that this long-running struggle will resume.

CHAPTER FOUR

Center Forward?
The Fate of the
New Democrats

Franklin Foer

THE 2000 DEMOCRATIC CONVENTION in Los Angeles seems another era ago, and that's because it was. If you were a New Democrat, it was a good time to be alive. Kenneth Baer's *Reinventing Democrats*, a history of the centrists' makeover of the party published on the eve of the convention, proclaimed, "No matter what happens in the year 2000, it is safe to assume that the DLC and the New Democrats will be at the center of any debate, or battle, to chart the future of the Democratic Party for the next century."

Based on all available evidence at the convention, that battle had already been settled. The mantle of the party had been handed from one of the Democratic Leadership Council's founding fathers, Bill Clinton, to another, Al Gore. That handover only begins to describe the reasons for believing that the reformers had triumphed and that the party's centrist wing had mastered and domesticated its coalition partners on the left. For his running mate, Gore tapped Joe Lieberman, a man with impeccable hawkish and culturally moderate credentials. The party's platform was written by a former editor of *Blueprint*, the DLC's journal. In its final version, the document had few of the McGovernite exhortations for reduced military spending and enforced busing that had crowded a generation of Democratic manifestos.

I spent that convention hanging out with New Democrats—attending their events and trailing after the movement's leading lights through the Staples Center and high-roller parties. Victory was theirs, and they knew it. Nearly every member of the party was self-identifying as a New Democrat those days. Even Jesse Jackson Jr., whose family had a long history of denouncing the DLC as racist and reactionary, had appeared on television to announce that he, too, was a New Democrat. As I made my way through the convention floor with Simon Rosenberg, the head of a fund-raising group called the New Democrat Network, I watched as he was swamped with candidates for Congress and state legislatures, all wanting to have his group's imprimatur.

Making our way through the Florida delegation, we encountered the head of the state's DLC, a gruff lawyer named Bob Grizzard. It should be said that Grizzard hardly possessed DLC president Al From's sense of Brooks Brothers sartorial style. Defiantly wearing a T-shirt from Clinton's 1992 campaign over a flannel shirt, Grizzard had announced to his delegation, "We're the party of diversity and inclusion . . . and if they don't want to swallow the DLC, we'll stick it to 'em." A minute later, he grabbed an African American member of the delegation and brought him over to us. "He's not quite with us yet," Grizzard laughed. "But give him time." Grizzard's friends seemed embarrassed by the gesture, but they shared his sense of centrist triumphalism. Bob Poe, Florida's party chair, told me, "The DLC is the wind in our sails."

From the perspective of the 2004 presidential race, it's hard not to feel that those early proclamations of triumph were premature. The centrist victory was either ephemeral or illusory. To start with the obvious: the 2004 campaign season witnessed the strange and troubling ascent of Howard Dean, a man who once proudly resided within the DLC but who ran for president by trumpeting distinctly uncentrist rhetoric. He promised to forcefully challenge the hegemony of the moderates. In speeches, he explicitly blasted the DLC and promised to represent the "Democratic wing of the Democratic Party"—a phrase that had first been invoked by Paul Wellstone and other Left-liberals who resisted the Clintonization of the party. For the centrists, the fact of Dean's campaign is this: the party came within a hair's breadth of handing the nomination to a man who had run one of the most Left campaigns in the party's history.

But Dean hardly represented the year's only instance of backsliding. The Edwards campaign gained surprising traction with his populist opposition to free trade agreements and his "Two Americas," us-versus-them stump speech. And it would be hard for a New Democrat to take too much solace in the ultimate triumph of John Kerry. Although Kerry has made some important feints in the direction of the DLC agenda over the course of his career—delivering speeches where he flirted with supporting vouchers and raising questions about affirmative action—he has never really been a stalwart of the movement. There are serious doubts as to his commitment to any core set of beliefs, let alone a heartfelt sympathy toward the New Democratic agenda.

In addition to the candidates, there are other questions about the health of the movement. For the first time since the late 1980s, the party's left wing has shown signs of life, and this actually understates the health of the Left. It isn't just stirring; it is vital, thanks to a proliferation of antiwar blogs, talk radio, and the unintended consequences of campaign finance reform, which have all exaggerated the power of unions, environmentalists, and other interest groups. The most troubling aspect of the Left's revival is its grim determination to imitate the Right. Where the Rush Limbaugh Right has spent the past decade being uncivil and mean, the Left's grassroots now demand that their party become more uncivil and mean, to match the wingnuts tit for tat.

Intellectually, the movement is on the defensive for the first time in many years. The Nobel Prize–winning economist Joseph Stiglitz, once a confident New Democrat, has raised some serious questions about the party's devotion to fiscal conservatism. "I believe we pushed deficit reduction too far," he wrote in his recent book *The Roaring Nineties*. "Unless we understand how to think about deficits, economic policies in the future will be distorted." Free trade has come up for serious discussion within the party, and it's not just a matter of political demagoguery. Although New Democrats touted the virtues of trade, they failed to seriously wrestle with the fallout from globalization.

What forces brought about the current moment of stagnation? How could this movement go so quickly from triumph to malaise? The answer, I think, is that triumph and malaise are deeply connected. Having succeeded in transforming the party and having implemented many of their most important reforms, they are stuck without a terribly coherent, compelling ideological mission. (Much of the time, the New Democrats seem as if they only exist to consolidate the gains their movement made in the 1980s and 1990s—not exactly inspiring stuff.) This is not to say that they don't have a crucial role in the party. Their flagship organization, the Democratic Leadership Council, and its think tank, the Progressive Policy Institute, continue to generate the soundest policy proposals in Washington. These two organizations draw on the movement's greatest virtue: its sensibility— a pragmatic, nonideological view of government that calls on the state to solve social ills only when social science evidence suggests that the state can do substantial good. As tacticians, they still have incredibly important insights. They are a necessary check on the party's left-wing kamikaze impulse to run full-throated, highly ideological campaigns. However, they don't have a clear mission or a strategy for revitalizing themselves.

What Were the New Democrats?

To describe the New Democratic mission, one must first describe the bleak landscape in which the movement sprang to life. The McGovern-Fraser reforms of 1971 were implemented to democratize the party; to take power away from the hands of crusty, old, white, male party apparatchiks; to move the nominating process from the smoky backrooms into the sunlight of the primary system. These reforms, of course, had an unintended consequence. Yes, the new system constituted a more open, more democratic process for selecting a nominee, but these primaries did not make the party a model of civic participation. Because primaries tended to inspire low turnout, their outcomes could be decided by the deployment of committed, organized bands of activists. In other words, in the context of Democratic Party politics, the candidate who could best tap the passions of the Left, the students, and the unions would win the primaries.

The transformation of the party was more thorough than these reforms, too. McGovern may have been pummeled in 1972, but his spirit triumphed two years later in the midterm elections, when a whole new generation of liberals came to Congress. Buoyed by a post-Watergate, throw-the-bums-out zeitgeist, they helped revolutionize the inner workings of Congress, overturning the seniority system that had long kept power in the hands of conservative Southern Democrats. The toothpaste was out of the tube. A whole genre of Democrats was displaced and disempowered by these changes.

It is important to remember that there were two constituent groups that were primed to join the New Democratic movement. First, and most obviously, there were the conservative and moderate Southern Democrats—your Sam Nunns and Chuck Robbs—who had been trampled by the party's social revolution. Second, there was a whole generation of Democratic Party intellectuals and wonks who were simply sick of losing elections and tired of the party's activist Left-liberal id triumphing over its tactical superego. They also believed that the class of 1974 and the other New Left–inspired rebels had created new orthodoxies within the party, preventing it from engaging in honest thinking about the efficacy and morality of its policies. These intellectuals figured themselves reformers; some of them even explicitly compared themselves to the progressives of the early twentieth century. Indeed, there is something to the analogy. For starters, they both viewed themselves as locked in combat against corrupt machines. Instead of fighting against the vulgar bosses who resided in city hall and party clubs, however, the New Democrats were fighting against a group of corrupt interest groups—the unions and the racial mau-mau artists.

When Richard Hofstadter described these early twentieth-century reformers, he portrayed them as denizens of a status-anxious middle class displaced in the new economy of the industrial age. The same could be said of the DLC, which represented a coalition of meritocrats and moderates dispossessed by the rise of the interest groups. And just like their progressive antecedents, the New Democrats represented the bourgeois counterattack. The New Democrats pushed for the party to embrace a middle-class ethic—"opportunity" and "responsibility" were omnipresent words in their slogans. In place of Keynesian profligacy, they proposed a program of fiscal restraint and fretted over deficits. On the cultural front, they wanted to beat back the libertinism of the 1960s, or the "adversarial culture," by more openly declaring their own religious faith and patriotism and embracing that of fellow citizens. They worried over teen pregnancy and modulated the party's rhetoric on abortion—"safe, legal, and rare" was their effective slogan.

More important than the movement's more conservative attitude toward the sexual revolution was its attitude toward work. Clinton and his fellow New Democrats recited lyrical paeons to old-fashioned industry. As a memo from Bruce Reed and Al Fromm put it, "Democrats need to show the middle class that we will honor their values, defend their country, and think twice before spending the tax dollars they worked so hard to earn." Thus, welfare reform became one of the single most important rallying cries of the movement.

There was a great strength to the New Democratic critique: they could devise a coherent ideology because their opponents on the left wing of the party had gone so far in the other direction. There was a lot to define them against: the New Left's takeover of the party had pushed it in such a leftward direction that Republicans didn't have to work hard to caricature Democratic candidates as "out-of-touch liberals," even if they were relatively moderate technocrats like Michael Dukakis.

Notwithstanding the appeal of the New Democrat approach, it is worth posing the obvious counterfactual question: Would the New Democrats have succeeded without Bill Clinton? There was an implacable logic to the reforms that the DLC proposed. The Democratic Party was going to become a hopeless, helpless minority if it didn't implement some major rhetorical and policy reforms. But the DLC was an unabashedly fratricidal organization. It rubbed the party's establishment the wrong way and precipitated a backlash. In 1985, the California congressional delegation more or less demanded that House Majority Whip Tony Coelho quit the organization. Jesse Jackson denounced the DLC as racist and corrupt, and plenty of others followed the good reverend in deriding the group as "Democrats for the Leisure Class." Barney Frank said, "The notion of being rescued by the right of the DLC is like being on the *Lusitania* and being told that the *Titanic* has been sent to rescue you." (On the flip side, William Galston and Elaine Kamarck charged the mainstream of the party with practicing "the politics of evasion" and "liberal fundamentalism.")[1]

Bill Clinton was the perfect vehicle for selling the New Democratic case to the party. With his rhetorical gifts, he somehow man-

1. William Galston and Elaine Ciulla Kamarck, "The Politics of Evasion: Democrats and the Presidency." Washington DC, Progressive Policy Institute, September 1989.

aged to sand down the edges of the DLC agenda. He added just the right modicum of populist rhetoric to his centrism—enough to convince Left-liberals that he might actually be one of them. To be sure, even Clinton couldn't really negotiate a rapprochement between the party's factions, as some of the bloody debates from his White House years illustrate. But if Clinton hadn't emerged in 1992, it seems clear that the party was set on an explosive course. There was no mechanism for arbitrating the increasingly vicious conflict between the two wings of the party. Perhaps another nominee—Paul Tsongas? Bob Kerrey?—would have been able to keep the party peace and prevent the Democrats from fracturing, but it seems unlikely.

What Are the New Democrats?

For all the virtues—both political and intellectual—that the New Democratic agenda has provided as a governing strategy, it hasn't fared nearly so well in opposition. Although Clinton endowed the party with a playbook, the party has been unable to score many points with it. Still clinging to the Clintonian middle ground, the Democrats were clobbered in the 2002 midterm election. Facing a disingenuous negotiating partner in George W. Bush, they have been made to look like fools in their legislative battles with the administration, where their good will toward the White House has never been reciprocated. The Left has attributed these problems to the weaknesses inherent in New Democratic thinking.

While the Left attacked them, the New Democrats faced their own internal identity crisis, which was evident in the 2004 campaign. Longtime stalwarts of the movement, like Elaine Kamarck, formerly of the Progressive Policy Institute, and Simon Rosenberg, head of the New Democrat Network, hitched themselves to the Dean campaign, even though Dean was explicitly campaigning against the DLC. The president of the DLC, Bruce Reed, became a primary adviser to the

Edwards campaign, even though Edwards spent most of the winter harping on the evils of free trade.

Over the past year, profound questions have arisen about what it means to be a New Democrat. What distinguishes the News Dems from the rest of the party? Are there clear issue cleavages, or just a tactical disagreement, or not even that? It's worth reexamining the original tenets of the movement to see how well they hold up, to measure how far the New Democratic agenda has progressed, and to find out how many—or few—fundamentals now separate the movement from the rest of the party.

Fiscal Conservatism

Even in the heyday of Rubinomics, when fiscal conservatism yielded undeniably handsome returns, there were Democratic dissidents, like Robert Kutner and Robert Reich, calling on the party to return to its Keynesian roots. But now, there are almost no Democrats in Washington who take this position—or at least no one who loudly takes this position. Congressional Democrats, even the most Left ones, have argued against the Bush tax cuts by charging it with fiscal irresponsibility. The old bastions of the Left, like the *Nation*, list the exploding budget deficit in their litany of Bush administration sins. Throughout the party, Rubinomics reigns supreme.

This new economic policy may be the greatest accomplishment of the New Democrats. It represents a fundamental reshaping of the party's attitude toward government. By placing limits on government spending, Rubinomics created de facto limits on the government programs that the party could support. But this success has come at a cost for the health of the movement because it has lost one of the primary rallying cries that distinguished it from the rest of the party.

Foreign Policy

During the 1980s, foreign policy clearly set the New Democrats apart. Sam Nunn, David Boren, and others cast an infinitely more skeptical eye toward arms control than the party's Left. They pushed for Congress to spend more on Reagan Doctrine proxies, like the Contras and the Afghan mujahadeen. In the 1990s, as the cold war melted away, foreign policy faded from the New Democratic agenda, too. Although New Democrats tended to favor the Gulf War and interventions in the Balkans, these issues weren't nearly as central as welfare reform and other domestic concerns.

Now that foreign policy has returned to its cold war importance, the New Democrats should return to their hawkish roots. Iraq has already led to a revival of the Left's old, latent antimilitarism. As the conflict continues, there will be a new generation of candidates who feel comfortable screaming, "Bring our troops home." It will fall to the New Democrats to prevent the Left's dovishness from reviving all the old worst stereotypes of the party's weakness. (It is incredible how the old stereotypes die so hard. Despite Clinton lobbing missiles into the Sudan and Afghanistan, and despite the Democratic Party's near unanimous support for interventions in Bosnia and Kosovo, the Democratic Party continues to pay a price for turning its back on its anticommunist traditions in the 1980s. To be sure, the old stereotypes persist because some old-style Democrats continue to make old-style arguments.)

Unfortunately, it's not an easy position to stake out. The New Democrats must split the difference between the revived McGovernite anti-imperialism of the Left and the robust unilaterialism of the Bush administration. In between, of course, there's plenty of room for a reasonable position: a greater sensitivity to multilateralism than the Bush administration has shown, a greater proclivity toward American power than felt by the Left. Unfortunately, it's not a position that lends itself to easily sellable slogans, let alone easily articulated principles. And what's worse, the New Democratic movement is largely devoid of foreign policy thinkers who might be able to tease out those slogans and principles. For a generation, the Democratic Party has bestowed power and prestige to domestic wonks, not foreign policy ones.

Race

More than any issue, race defined the rise of the New Democrats in the 1980s. This issue clearly represented the party's Achilles heel. For its support of affirmative actions and busing, the Democratic Party suffered twenty years of white working-class backlash. If Democrats couldn't find a way to blunt the Republicans' tapping of racial anxieties, they would continue to reel from Willie Horton–like attacks. To reverse these trends, the New Democrats proposed a series of maneuvers, both subtle and blunt. In addition to expressing their displeasure with affirmative action, they picked fights with Jesse Jackson, trying to lower his stock within the party. A 1991 DLC conference famously snubbed Jackson while inviting others from the Left.

But race is another example of how Clinton managed to both score a decisive victory for the New Democrats and blur their identity. By enacting welfare reform and staking out his mend-it-don't-end-it position on affirmative action, he managed to artfully diffuse the white backlash against the Democratic Party. States like Georgia and Ohio suddenly became winnable for the party.

With this new consensus on race, New Democrats don't have any tactical grounds for urging their heartfelt opposition to affirmative action. In addition, with this new consensus on race, the environment doesn't lend itself to talking openly and honestly about the New Democrats' positions on the issue.

Populism

In the postmortems of the 2000 election, the New Democrats were able to easily posit a theory for Al Gore's defeat. Gore had lost by reverting to class warfare rhetoric of old-fashioned Democratic populism, thus alienating the white men in the middle who swung the election. The debates over the Gore debacle were a continuation of a decades-long blood feud that had pitted the DLC against the labor movement and its intellectual defenders. That's why it is such a shock to now see the DLC beginning to embrace the very populist rhetoric that it had attacked for so long. What's the evidence of this reconciliation with populism? It was visible in the John Edwards campaign, where the DLC's president Bruce Reed and other major movement figures helped formulate a message that complained about "two Americas" and that railed against corporations, free trade agreements, and an economy that rewarded "wealth over work." DLC memos actually treated populism as an acceptable fact of Democratic Party politics.

What can explain this turn around? For one thing, I think the DLC has shifted a few steps to the Left since the 2000 campaign. Reed, one of the great wonks of his generation, has less taste for the internecine fighting that characterized the old debates over populism. Also, the Bush administration has, in part, changed the reality of the American economy. He really has tilted the system in favor of corporations and the wealthy. His policies really do cry out for populist critique.

The DLC's willingness to embrace populism represents the new spirit of rapprochement that permeates the movement and the party in the wake of the presidential primaries. Examples abound of this growing Democratic unity. New Democrats have been invited into meetings with the liberal interest groups, where the 527 organizations coordinate and plot strategy. Centrists who were blackballed from the *American Prospect* have since been hired as columnists.

Tactics

Without substantial policy differences separating the New Democrats from the Old, the movement's most defining characteristic is its tactical approach—the strategy that the Clinton campaigns deployed in the 1990s. Whereas Old Democrats urge the party to increase its electoral tally by investing in efforts to turn out blacks, unions, and other Left-liberal voters, New Democrats have tried to push the party to appeal to uncommitted voters in the middle. Of course, there's an ideological subtext to this division: the Old Democrats believe that turnout can be boosted by running a campaign that strokes all the Left's erogenous zones. Even if such raw liberalism will turn off some swing voters, the argument goes, that loss will be more than compensated for with the invigorated Left-liberals who will swarm the polls. Conversely, the significance of the DLC's focus on swing voters is that the only way to reach the voters in the center is to downplay the party's left-liberalism and recraft its image to make it more palatable to middle America.

Before the late 1990s, it was very difficult to muster an argument against the DLC's strategy. The numbers clearly showed that elections couldn't be won just by turning out the base. But that began to change. With the Gingrich revolution, the impeachment of Bill Clinton, and the contested result of the 2000 election, the nation became increasingly polarized along partisan lines. The slice of voters in the middle has become much thinner. Clearly, this is the way that Karl Rove and the Bush administration view the electorate. Starting in 2001, Rove began touting an essay by Michael Barone on the 50–50 nation—an electorate split evenly in its allegiances. Consequently, Rove has argued that the election will be determined by the administration's ability to turn out its conservative vote. To achieve this goal, he told an American Enterprise Institute seminar in 2001 that he wanted to boost Bush's harvest of evangelical votes by four million. A similar strain of logic has propelled the administration to focus on steel tariffs to appease steelworkers in Pennsylvania and West Virginia. The administration views the election as so inevitably tight that it must be won on the margins, not by broadcasting a message aimed at broad swaths of voters.

This view of the electorate—closely divided, with margins of victory decided by the turnout of the base—has also found a new widespread following within the Democratic Party. This was the theory of Howard Dean and his guru, Joe Trippi. During the campaign, they frequently cited the work of the Berkeley linguist George Lakoff and his book, *Moral Politics*, on the potential for progressive mobilization. "What you do is crank the heck out of your base, get them really excited and crank up the base turnout and you'll win the middle-of-the-roaders," Dean told *U.S. News*'s Roger Simon.

Even if the DLC has exhausted its policy ideas—and I'm not saying it has—it would be worth having the DLC around simply to block the Democrats from embracing this tight view of the electorate. For starters, just because Rove talks about turning out evangelical voters does not mean he will ignore the middle. The whole initial stage of the Bush 2004 campaign has been about creating an image of John Kerry in swing voters' minds, scaring them into believing that he is weak on national security and an entirely untrustworthy flip-flopper. Second, the data just don't support the Left's view of the electorate. About one-third of all voters are hard-core Democrats, and about 10 percent more usually vote Democratic. So even if every one of them voted, you would still need an additional 7 to 10 percent of the electorate to win, and this may overcount the partisans. A 2004 study by the Pew Research Center classified 29 percent of the voters as swing voters.

This isn't to say that the DLC has always gotten things right. They have tended to embrace hokey concepts to precisely pinpoint the identity of the swing voters whom they insist the party must target. Remember the "Wired Dads," the worker bees who populated suburban office parks, the group the DLC's pollster Mark Penn trumpeted in the 2000 election? Still, they do have the right general idea.

What Will Be a New Democrat?

In defining the New Democrats throughout this essay, I've used the term "movement." It's a term I use because that's the way the New Democrats describe themselves. But in a sense, this word doesn't fit all that comfortably. The New Democrats never really had local members or any of the other characteristics that constitute true social movements. On the contrary, the DLC is an insiders' group that focuses its efforts mostly on politicians in Washington—not on the people who put them there. This is a big problem. Like the neoconservatives and libertarians, indeed like all but a few ideological movements in modern American politics, the New Democrats have failed to develop a mass constituency for their ideas.

Even though they might not be a mass movement, however, the New Democrats are undeniably an intellectual movement. Even if they are confined to a few offices on Capitol Hill, they continue to serve an important function. Despite the emergence of the Center for American Progress, the Progressive Policy Institute continues to be one of the few deeply wonky generators of Democratic ideas. On trade and education, most notably, and in other areas, too, the PPI actually produces original, detailed proposals for new initiatives. When they don't produce new initiatives, they often produce clever rhetorical strategies for selling old ones—or solid, highly sellable arguments for challenging Republican proposals.

Could the New Democrats ever transform themselves into a mass movement? Obviously, people don't usually take to the streets calling for sensible incrementalist changes in government—Education Reform! Reinventing Government! The People United! Still, there seems to be far more potential for cultivating the segment of the electorate that is alienated by both Left and Right. So far in this essay, I've provided one big reason why the DLC hasn't been able to further expand its political base to provide a home for these people. To paraphrase Richard Hofstadter's description of third parties, the New Democrats stung and then they faded. They achieved their biggest goals and then lost much of their vitality.

There are several additional reasons why they haven't revived themselves as an important force within the party. First, they suffer from a rather debilitating case of Clinton nostalgia. Of course, nearly everyone in the party suffers from a debilitating case of Clinton nostalgia, but this syndrome seems to afflict New Democrats more than anyone else. Instead of formulating their next set of issues and ideas, they often find themselves occupied with defending the Clinton legacy against attacks from the Left and the Right. When they aren't defending the Clinton record, they are touting it as a model of how their centrist strategy can enable Democrats to successfully run government and the party. All this time spent fighting and defending the last war means they have been less than effective in preparing for the next one.

Second, they have managed to squander the rhetoric and politics of reform. In a sense, the origins of the New Democrats trace back to Gary Hart, Tim Wirth, their fellow neoliberals, and the heyday of the *Washington Monthly*. These proto–New Democrats had one major clarion call: to reform the bureaucracies that inefficiently implemented social policy. This mantle of reform had been prominently displayed in the Clinton campaigns and his administrations: "reinventing government" was an omnipresent idea, as were welfare and education reform. Like all the best New Democratic ideas, these three were simultaneously good politics and good policy. They helped dispel the deeply held beliefs that the Democratic Party existed for the sole purpose of growing the bureaucracy.

However, those old reformist hobbyhorses no longer exist. Welfare reform has been accomplished. Campaign finance was overhauled. Bush adopted and then bungled the New Democrats' education agenda. And though reinventing government might still be good policy, it has lost its political novelty. The New Democrats need to propose a new set of policies that could help revivify the concept of reform. John Kerry has a few decent reformist ideas, such as his suggestions for the tax system, but there's not enough out there to justify a whole new reformist rhetoric that could be politically and intellectually powerful. Without this broader rhetorical and intellectual framework, the DLC will have a hard time being more than a centrist think tank and the New Democrats will have a hard time being a social movement.

Third, the New Democrats need to start doing more foreign policy thinking. Their silence on the issue is deafening. If they felt as passionately about international issues as they do about domestic ones, they would be doing more to press Kerry. They would be deriding him for retreating from his commitment to Iraqi democracy; they would be pushing him to level more sweeping critiques of the Bush administration's failure to follow through on its rhetorical paeons to democracy in the Middle East. The administration's continued closeness to Saudi Arabia, as always, should be a prime concern. It's hard to imagine the New Democrats will ever regain their importance if they can't speak forcefully about the greatest issue of our times.

One Last Rhetorical Question, Posed and Answered

You might ask: If the New Democrats have triumphed in so many areas and if they can't easily articulate a coherent agenda, then why should they bother trying to do more than produce ideas and policies? The answer lies on the left. Bush has inspired a new wave of radicalism on the party's liberal flank. There's no better evidence of this than the elevated stature of Michael Moore.

For a Democratic politician, there should be no obvious upside in identifying with Michael Moore. During the last election, he dumped all over the party, lending his full-throated endorsement to Ralph Nader's candidacy. After September 11, he cast his lot with the radicals again, opposing the American war in Afghanistan. And now, he has put together a movie that confirms all the cheapest anti-American slurs, as well as spinning irresponsible conspiracies. You would think that these positions would make Moore political poison.

But Moore hasn't been political poison—or at least he hasn't been treated like political poison. Starting in the primaries, the Democrats rushed to embrace him. General Wesley Clark campaigned with him in the New Hampshire primary. The party's leadership turned out to the red carpet premiere of his film *Fahrenheit 9/11* at Washington's Uptown Theater. Here's Tom Daschle; there's Terry McAuliffe extending his arm to the burly documentarian.

Right now, it's hard to consider the Left too grave a threat to the future of the party. For the time being, they seem to be in an incredibly pragmatic mood, driven by an overwhelming, earnest determination to oust Bush. But what happens if Kerry loses? I'm guessing that the proponents of the old left-liberal style of campaigning will announce that events have vindicated their view of the world. They will pin blame for the defeat on Kerry's "cautious" style and his "centrist" view. And if the Left claims to champion bare-knuckled politics now, just watch how bloody the election postmortems will be. It is at that moment that we'll need the New Democrats to defend their policy legacy, their political playbook, and all that is sensible in the party. We'll need them more than ever.

PART III

The Future of Progressivism

What's a Progressive to Do? Strategies for Social Reform in a Hostile Political Climate

David Cole

AMERICAN PROGRESSIVES SEEKING social justice face a real dilemma in the current political climate. In prior periods, they looked to the president, the Congress, or the courts to advance their agenda. The New Deal administration of Franklin Delano Roosevelt, the Democratic Congress of the 1960s, 1970s, and 1980s, and the Warren Court of the 1950s and 1960s each offered significant opportunities for instituting progressive social reforms. Today, however, progressives face a hostile president, a hostile Congress, and a hostile Supreme Court. There is literally nowhere to turn. What is a progressive to do?

In this essay, I seek to address one specific iteration of this question—namely, what is progressivism's relation to law at the turn of the twenty-first century? As Alexis de Tocqueville observed almost 200 years ago, in the United States, most political disputes inevitably evolve into legal disputes. Given this apparently inescapable fact of (at least American) life, the relationship between progressivism and law is a critical issue. And ever since the NAACP Legal Defense and Educational Fund's victory in *Brown v. Board of Education*, progressives have often looked to the courts, to lawyers, and to litigation as principal tools in achieving social justice.

The progressive's relationship to law has changed markedly over the past fifty years. This change has had both substantive and tactical components. On the substantive level, progressives have been compelled to hone their claims for justice. Bold assertions of social and economic rights, and of substantive equality in general, have given way to more limited claims of equal *opportunity*. Instead of seeking to define and protect affirmative rights, progressives have argued that, at least where the state protects rights, those rights should be defined and implemented in such a way that they are enjoyed equally by all. At the same time, the language of rights has been buttressed by the language of social costs and benefits. Progressives have increasingly framed arguments for rights in utilitarian terms, arguing that denying basic rights ultimately imposes substantial costs on the majority. These substantive redefinitions of rights (and of the justifications for rights) are, in part, a grudging acknowledgment that the broader claims have less appeal these days, especially in court; but they are also more than that. The redefinitions constitute a recognition that achieving equality through law poses serious challenges to other progressive values, such as liberty and democracy. As a result, equality, the central normative commitment of progressives, demands a more nuanced and qualified approach. At the same time, the progressive's reliance on utilitarian and pragmatic arguments reflects an important lesson about the need to appeal to a broad audience in order to achieve real change.

At the tactical level, progressives have proposed a variety of strategies for coping with hostile courts. All agree that federal court litigation is no longer the primary source of social change. Some, such as Mark Tushnet, have argued that the Constitution should be "taken away from the courts," questioning the notion that courts should have the final say on what the Constitution means.[1] Other progressives

---

1. Mark Tushnet, *Taking the Constitution Away From the Courts* (Princeton, NJ: Princeton University Press, 1999).

have looked to state courts and legislatures when federal reforms have failed. Perhaps the most widely shared conclusion of the past fifty years is that courts are unlikely to be the centerpiece of a progressive reform strategy; instead, courts should be seen as one tool among many in what must be a multitiered effort to achieve social change.

A promising avenue for progressives that has been less broadly explored is presented by the era of globalization, in which domestic issues may be linked to global ones and global attention may be brought to bear on domestic concerns. Progressive advocates may increasingly need to look outward in order to make progress at home. Americans have often thought of international human rights as addressing other nation's problems and have paid little attention to comparative constitutional law, assuming that our constitutional doctrine sets the benchmark for all others. But if this view was ever justified, it is becoming less and less so. This is particularly so where the international community has advanced beyond American law. Thus, progressives should employ international human rights law, fora, and tactics to press for social reform on the domestic front.

While many of the substantive and tactical changes described below have been necessitated by hostility to progressive values from the three branches of the federal government, and especially from the courts, the need to adapt has, in my view, made progressivism stronger and smarter. Honing arguments against formidable foes often forces one to make one's arguments better. Because of that challenge, the lessons learned from the past fifty years of struggle have left progressives better situated to advance social reform in the fifty years to come.

The Old and the New

In the old days, everything was so much simpler (or so it seems in retrospect). For years, the NAACP Legal Defense and Education Fund's classic strategy for dismantling segregation in the South was the gold standard of progressive legal reform efforts. In the 1960s and 1970s, progressive activists increasingly became public interest lawyers and formed organizations devoted to using courts to push social change. Women's rights advocates, led by Ruth Ginsburg working on behalf of the ACLU's Women's Rights Project, carefully crafted a strategy to educate the Supreme Court about sex discrimination, leading to the Court's adoption of heightened scrutiny for sex-based classifications.[2] Progressive movements came to be defined in terms of group rights—immigrants' rights, children's rights, disability rights, gay rights, and so forth.

The source of, and inspiration for, this vision was the Supreme Court under Chief Justice Earl Warren. During Warren's tenure, from 1953 to 1969, and continuing for a substantial part of Chief Justice Warren Burger's tenure, from 1969 to 1986, the Supreme Court was, in fact, a significant force for progressive social change. The Court declared an end to de jure segregation, aggressively advanced the rights of African Americans, radically expanded the concept of privacy and the rights of criminal suspects and defendants, and declared sex discrimination presumptively invalid. It sought to implement broad-based structural reform through decisions like *Brown v. Board of Education*, barring segregated public education, and *Miranda v. Arizona* and *Gideon v. Wainwright*, which extended the right to a lawyer, paid for by the state, to all indigent persons under interrogation or indictment in the criminal system.

Law professors wrote books and articles extolling the role of courts in implementing social change. Although published a decade after Chief Justice Warren's resignation, John Hart Ely's *Democracy and Distrust*, inspired by that Court's work, offered a sustained and compelling intellectual rationale for the Warren Court approach.[3] Ely

2. See David Cole, "Strategies of Difference: Litigating for Women's Rights in a Man's World," *Journal of Law & Inequality* 2 (1984): 33.

3. John Hart Ely, *Democracy and Distrust* (Cambridge, MA: Harvard University Press, 1980).

argued that federal courts, as countermajoritarian institutions in a liberal democracy, served their highest purpose when they protected the political process from itself by zealously safeguarding those rights critical to a functioning democracy, in particular the First Amendment and the right to vote, and by protecting those who could not protect themselves through the political process, in particular, "discrete and insular minorities." In 1976 and 1979, Abram Chayes and Owen Fiss wrote influential articles in the *Harvard Law Review* arguing that courts should be understood not merely as adjudicators of private disputes but also as appropriate forums for "public law litigation" seeking systemic institutional reform.[4]

But just as the ideas of Ely, Fiss, and Chayes were taking hold in law schools, Ronald Reagan was elected president of the United States, and everything changed. Reagan aggressively attacked "judicial activism" and appointed hundreds of federal judges committed to a conservative agenda and hostile to the kind of judicially mandated institutional reform that progressives had learned to love. The first President Bush continued this effort. Facing a Republican Congress for much of his tenure, President Clinton chose not to fight back in the field of judicial appointments and instead nominated mostly moderate judges who were not committed to a progressive agenda for social change. The second President Bush revived the ideological litmus test appointments of President Reagan, and although Democrats in the Senate have used the filibuster to block several of Bush's most extreme nominees, the vast majority of his judicial appointments have been confirmed.

As a result, progressive lawyers today face a legal landscape radically altered from the one their counterparts faced in the 1960s and 1970s. The Republicans control the White House and Congress, and, as President Clinton's tenure showed, a Democratic president with a

---

4. Owen Fiss, "The Forms of Justice," *Harvard Law Review* 93 (1979): 1; Abram Chayes, "The Role of the Judge in Public Law Litigation," *Harvard Law Review* 89 (1976): 1281.

Republican Congress is sharply limited in his ability to achieve social progress. The Supreme Court today consists of three radically conservative Justices (Rehnquist, Scalia, and Thomas), two traditional conservatives (Kennedy and O'Connor), and four moderates (Stevens, Souter, Ginsburg, and Breyer). With the possible exception of Justice Souter, the Court has no justice today as liberal as Justices Warren, Blackmun, Douglas, Brennan, or Marshall. On most controversial issues, the conservative bloc prevails, as it did, most notably by blocking the Florida recount to ensure that George W. Bush would be elected president. A "victory" for progressives in the Supreme Court these days consists largely of holding on to prior gains (e.g., the 2003 decision not to declare all affirmative action in education unconstitutional and the 2001 decision not to reverse *Miranda*). The lower courts are also composed predominantly of conservative and moderate judges.

At the same time, outside the area of gay rights, many of the most extreme and explicit examples of injustice and discrimination have already been addressed, leaving in their wake a wide range of subtler and more difficult issues. For example, de jure racial segregation, explicit sex-based barriers to economic and educational opportunities, and race-based selection of criminal juries have all been barred. Profound problems of race, sex, and class-based inequality remain, but they take forms that are usually less explicit and more daunting to remedy.

In the face of these more systemic problems, the courts have grown skeptical of judicially managed institutional reform. In significant part, this skepticism reflects the increasingly conservative bent of federal judges, but it also reflects the legendary difficulties confronted in the effort to dismantle racial segregation. The implementation of *Brown v. Board of Education* has been much criticized, and although there are no longer formal racial barriers in public education, segregated education remains a persistent fact of life throughout the United States. Judicial oversight over desegregation orders has sometimes lasted for more than three decades, often without much apparent progress. In part, this failure can be attributed to the Supreme Court's unwillingness to take on de facto segregation and its refusal to permit interdistrict remedies, thereby making it nearly impossible to address the phenomenon of white flight to the suburbs. In part, however, it has to do with the entrenched reality of racial inequity and segregation in our society. Residential segregation, for example, plays a significant role in much public school segregation these days, but apart from a largely unsuccessful effort with busing, the courts have, for the most part, been unwilling to address the effects of residential segregation on public education.

Sometimes the courts appear to fear "too much justice," as Justice Brennan put it in a dissent in a death penalty case in 1987. In that case, *McCleskey v. Kemp*,[5] the defendant's lawyers commissioned a sophisticated statistical study of the administration of the death penalty in Georgia and found that even after controlling for thirty-nine potentially correlated nonracial variables, a defendant who killed a white victim was 4.3 times more likely to receive the death penalty than a defendant whose victim was black. The Court rejected McCleskey's claim that these racial effects rendered imposition of the death penalty discriminatory or cruel and unusual. The Court said that for McCleskey to prevail, he would have had to show not merely systemwide disparities but also discriminatory intent specific to his personal case. The Court noted that were it to rule otherwise, the entire criminal justice system might be called into question because race and sex disparities can be found in the administration of many, if not most, criminal laws. The Court's analysis was plainly driven by its sense that the problem presented was larger than the Court could possibly handle; therefore, it defined it as not a constitutional problem.

These days, rights discourse is used as often to stifle progressive

5. 481 U.S. 279 (1987).

reform as to facilitate it. Challengers claim that race-based affirmative action violates equal protection, that environmental regulations intrude on property rights, that campaign finance reform and laws governing corporations violate First Amendment speech rights, and that federal statutes—such as the Age Discrimination in Employment Act, the Americans With Disabilities Act, the Family and Medical Leave Act, the Violence Against Women Act, and the Religious Freedom Restoration Act—designed to extend rights to various groups, intrude impermissibly on states' rights. As in the *Lochner v. New York*[6] era, when the Supreme Court relied on states' rights, rights of contract, and rights of property to invalidate progressive economic legislation designed to protect workers from exploitation, the language of rights today all too often operates as an impediment to, rather than a catalyst for, social change.

Normative Adjustments

The reality described above presents significant obstacles to any campaign for progressive social reform through law. That fact has led to a number of shifts in progressive thinking and activism. Those shifts can be seen as both substantive, in the sense of changing what progressives ask for, and tactical, or changing the means employed to achieve what progressives want. This division is, in some sense, artificial, for the relationship between substantive demands and tactical strategies is dynamic. The means available for change often dictate how much one can ask for. A civil rights bill introduced in a Congress controlled by Democrats will necessarily look very different from a civil rights bill introduced in a Republican Congress, even if the bill is introduced by the same member of Congress with the support of the same civil rights groups. In some sense, all reform efforts today— whether legislative, executive, or judicial—must contend with the real-

---

6. *Lochner v. New York*, 198 U.S. 45 (1905); see also Cass R. Sunstein, "Lochner's Legacy," *Columbia Legal Review* 87 (1987): 873.

ity of limited possibilities. It is nonetheless useful to identify both changes in the ends sought and means chosen to further progressive reform.

Asking for Less

The most important normative commitment of progressives is to equality. But equality is not self-defining. In the heyday of the Warren Court, progressives argued for "substantive equality" over "formal equality," by which they meant not merely the elimination of formal race and sex-based barriers but also the elimination of practices, even facially neutral practices, that have the *effect* of maintaining or increasing racial, sexual, or class-based subordination. According to this view, if a race-neutral college admissions policy leads to underrepresentation of black students, the progressive commitment to equality not only permits but also *demands* that the college adopt admissions standards that remedy that underrepresentation. Had this view of equal protection prevailed, race-based affirmative action would be not only permissible but also mandatory, as long as, in the absence of affirmative action, minorities were underrepresented.

Similarly, progressives in the past often advocated an affirmative, rather than a negative, understanding of rights. The right to engage in a certain activity should entail not only the negative right to stop the government from interfering with the exercise of the right but also the affirmative right to government assistance where, absent that assistance, the right cannot be exercised. The right to counsel in criminal cases is an example of an affirmative right: the state bears the obligation to permit criminal defendants to bring their own paid lawyer into court and to appoint a lawyer, at the state's expense, if the defendant is indigent and cannot afford to hire a lawyer. However, the right to counsel is a rare exception to the norm. In general, courts have been reluctant to view rights as affirmative. More typical is the Supreme Court's ruling that Medicaid programs need not fund abortions, even though the result in practice is that only women with access to adequate resources have a meaningful right to terminate their pregnancy.[7] The right to privacy, the Court insisted, barred the state from interfering with a woman's choice but did not require it to fund her choice.

Progressives in the past also advocated economic and social rights, in addition to civil and political rights. They argued that the rights to speak, associate, and vote do not mean very much if you don't have food to eat, clothes to wear, or a roof over your head. Rights to public education, shelter, health care, and child care are all forms of economic and social rights. Notably, none of these rights is expressly guaranteed in the U.S. Constitution, although constitutions of other countries (and of some of the fifty states) do guarantee some forms of social and economic rights. State constitutions, for example, often guarantee a right to an adequate or effective public education.

Each of these conceptions of justice has largely failed to take root in American constitutional jurisprudence. Courts have been reluctant to take on the difficult questions of how one defines such concepts as "substantive equality," "affirmative rights," and "social and economic rights." What is the appropriate baseline, for example, for measuring underrepresentation of minorities in a particular college? How much does the state have to pay to provide its indigent citizens with an "affirmative right" such as the right to counsel? And how would a court define a "right to health care"? Must everyone have access to a doctor, the specialist of his or her choice, or the best in the field?

Affirmative rights, substantive equality, and social and economic rights also pose real difficulties of implementation. The right to counsel provides an excellent example of these difficulties. As noted above, in this one area, the Court has guaranteed an affirmative right. As countless reports and studies have shown, however, the Court has

7. *Harris v. McRae*, 448 U.S. 297 (1980); *Maher v. Roe*, 432 U.S. 464 (1977).

failed to make this right a meaningful one. While the Court requires criminal legal assistance to be "effective," its standard for effectiveness is so low that most indigent defendants do not receive competent counsel with sufficient resources to defend them adequately. Courts have found no violation of the right to counsel, even when indigent defendants have been represented by lawyers with no prior experience in criminal law; by lawyers who have been drunk, on drugs, or asleep during portions of the trial; and by lawyers paid no more than $2,000 for all their out-of-court work on a death penalty trial.[8] The fact is that society has been unwilling to pay what it would cost to provide truly effective lawyers to the indigent, and the courts have been unwilling to require society to do so.

Thus, claims for substantive equality, affirmative rights, and social and economic rights have not fared well, and progressives have been forced to reframe their normative demands. A more limited line of progressive legal argument appeals not to abstract and absolute demands of equality, nor to affirmative or economic rights, but to the obligation to define rights equally for all. For example, I have argued that within the criminal justice system, however one strikes the balance between protecting liberty and privacy from state intrusion and affording the police sufficient authority to protect the citizenry from criminals, the balance ought to be struck in the same place for all.[9] We ought not protect a more robust conception of privacy for the rich than for the poor or for the white majority than for racial minority groups. Everyone should have the same rights to privacy and liberty, regardless of class or skin color. Similarly, in the area of national security, we ought not strike the balance between liberty and security by imposing on foreign nationals burdens and obligations that the citizenry does not equally share, at least with respect to basic rights like the right not to be detained arbitrarily, the right to due process,

8. David Cole, *No Equal Justice: Race and Class in the American Criminal Justice System* (New York: New Press, 1999), 63–100.
9. Ibid.

and the freedoms of speech and association.[10] Such arguments insist that we spread the cost evenly so that the majority has a stake equal to that of the minority in the rights at issue.

These arguments suppose that in a democracy, the majority is unlikely to be willing to impose onerous burdens upon itself except where those burdens are truly necessary. By closing off the option of imposing the costs selectively on a vulnerable minority for the benefit (or perceived benefit) of the majority, they seek to force the polity to strike the balance fairly. Once that escape route is blocked, this approach surmises, the political process is much more likely to get the balance right because everyone's interests will be taken into account on both sides of the scale. Thus, for example, after September 11, the increased security measures at airports, which affect all travelers, were adopted with careful attention to not imposing too much indignity, cost, or time on travelers. By contrast, the preventive detention campaign undertaken after September 11, which eventually rounded up some 5,000 foreign nationals in antiterrorism initiatives, was fraught with egregious rights violations, including secret arrests and hearings, denial of access to lawyers, arrests without charges, detention without hearings, and physical abuse. The tactics employed against the 5,000 foreign nationals likely would not have been possible had they been applied more broadly, especially to citizens. Thus, insisting that sacrifices in rights be shared equally is likely to ensure that the sacrifices will be less extreme and more carefully justified and implemented.

Progressive campaign finance reform also appeals to the notion that people should have an equal right to exercise their rights. The movement is predicated on the notion that the constitutional ideal of "one person, one vote" is threatened by unlimited use of money in political campaigns. Money corrupts the political process by essentially

10. David Cole, *Enemy Aliens: Double Standards and Constitutional Freedoms in the War on Terrorism* (New York: New Press, 2003).

giving those with substantial resources more than "one vote." There-fore, progressives argue, it is essential to regulate campaign spending to ensure equality in the right to choose one's representatives. This debate, like the arguments about equality in the criminal justice and national security areas outlined above, also has an instrumental aspect. If the democratic process truly provides equal representation, then the majority will have a greater opportunity to insist that the privileged elite share some of their resources through more redistributive taxing and spending policies.

The gay rights movement also couches its arguments in terms of the right to enjoy equally the rights that others already enjoy. The gay marriage controversy involves the claim that same-sex couples should have the same right to marry that different-sex couples have. In addition, the successful 2003 Supreme Court challenge to a Texas antisodomy statute argued, in part, that gays and lesbians have a right to sexual intimacy equal to that enjoyed by heterosexuals.[11]

Thus, in a variety of settings, progressive arguments have shifted from grand claims of substantive equality, affirmative rights, and social and economic rights to more limited claims that rights enjoyed by some should be equally enjoyed by all. To be sure, progressives have not given up entirely on the more ambitious notions of equality and rights, but they have acknowledged that these more ambitious con-ceptions of equality pose substantial costs, both in terms of liberty—because they require affording substantial power to government—and in terms of administrability—because they pose extremely challenging line-drawing decisions not readily susceptible to principled resolution. Not all progressives have given up on the more ambitious understand-ing of equality, but even those who retain those commitments have largely abandoned the pursuit of them through the courts.

11. *Lawrence v. Texas*, 123 S. Ct. 2476 (2003).

Rights in a Utilitarian and Pragmatic Frame

Progressives have also shifted the focus of their normative arguments about rights, both in courts and in the public arena. Reverend Martin Luther King Jr. spoke in terms of absolute ideals and basic conceptions of justice. Although today's progressives sometimes invoke the rhetoric of Dr. King, they are just as apt to add more utilitarian arguments for rights. Thus, not only do defenders of a living wage or equal educational opportunity argue that these are the right things to do to respect human dignity and to meet the demands of equality, but they also frequently maintain that inequality in these areas imposes substantial costs on society as a whole. Inadequate education, for example, fails to prepare citizens for the demands of the working world and results in a less productive workforce and a less healthy economy. Likewise, denying basic living assistance to poor children may lead to substantial health problems that will eventually be borne by society at large. Having the highest incarceration rate in the world is costly in terms of the outlays required to house people for decades, as well as the devastating effect incarceration has on inmates' job and career prospects upon release. This, in turn, may lead to recidivism, which imposes further costs on the community at large.

These arguments appear to have some traction. For example, arguments about the economic importance of providing everyone with an adequate public education have generally proved more successful in spurring educational finance reform than more absolutist claims about rights to equality. Arguments about the costs, both direct and indirect, of mass incarceration have led the public to favor reductions in criminal sentences. What unites such appeals is that they seek to show that while denials of rights may seem to save on costs in the short run, they have the effect of increasing costs for all in the long run. In this way, progressive advocates appeal to the self-interest of the majority and of privileged elites as a way to justify upholding rights of the minority and the disempowered.

This form of argument is especially visible in the area of national security and civil liberties after the terrorist attacks of September 11. While civil liberties advocates (of which I am one) often appeal to the public's sense of basic justice and human rights, they also argue that the deprivation of liberties actually makes us less secure. For example, the response to the horrifying images of torture inflicted on Iraqi detainees at Abu Ghraib prison was twofold. First, of course, advocates insisted that the guards' behavior was shameful, immoral, and wrong. This moral condemnation was often coupled with a second claim about the deleterious effects the conduct would have on the progress of the U.S. war on terror. The Abu Ghraib scandal is now widely seen as having dealt a devastating blow to U.S. efforts because it fostered resentment against the United States. In turn, that resentment made potential allies less eager to cooperate with us and provided recruiting incentives for al Qaeda and other terrorist groups that have turned their attention on us.

This latter contention illustrates a critically important utilitarian and pragmatic defense of rights; namely, rights play a crucial role in fostering the legitimacy of any official enterprise. If the justice system is seen as legitimate, for example, authorities will find less need to resort to force because people are much more likely to comply with legal regimes that they view as legitimate. Similarly, if the U.S. response to terrorism is seen as measured, careful, and respectful of human rights and the rule of law, cooperation from the rest of the world would be much more forthcoming and the threats we face would be much more likely to diminish. If, by contrast, we adopt methods that are seen as illegitimate, our enterprise will be compromised in fundamental ways, requiring more reliance on hard power rather than "soft power"; on force rather than consent.

These arguments reflect a recognition that in the modern era, absolutist claims are received more skeptically, and therefore appeals to cost, to self-interest, and to the majority's well-being are increasingly important. This is not to say that progressives have abandoned, or should abandon, appeals to moral principle. Principles such as equality, autonomy, liberty, and privacy remain powerful ideals in the American grain. But progressives increasingly seek to buttress those more absolutist appeals with utilitarian and pragmatic claims that the protection of rights, over the long run, is actually in the best interest of the whole community.

Different Strategies

In addition to adjusting their normative claims and arguments, progressive lawyers, scholars, and activists have proposed a variety of changes in strategy to adapt to the reality of a predominantly hostile federal judiciary, headed by a very conservative Supreme Court. The reactions have varied from advocating abandonment of the courts to shifts to state courts. Some reactions make more sense than others, but all share a recognition that we aren't going to see many decisions like *Brown v. Board of Education* and *Miranda v. Arizona* from the U.S. Supreme Court in the foreseeable future. Therefore, progressives have no choice but to think about and pursue alternative strategies.

Taking the Constitution Away From the Courts

One response of progressives to their inhospitable audience in the federal judiciary has been to look to the other branches of government, or to the people themselves, as a locus for advancing constitutional values. Professors Mark Tushnet, Larry Sager, and Robert Post have all argued, in varying degrees, that our understanding of the Constitution is too court-centric. Sager and Post maintained that because of the courts' institutional limitations, many constitutional norms are likely to be underenforced by courts.[12] Doctrinal limits on

---

12. Larry Sager, "Fair Measure: The Legal Status of Underenforced Constitutional Norms," *Harvard Law Review* 91 (1978): 1212; Robert Post, "Legislative Constitutionalism and Section Five Power: Policentric Interpretation of the Family and Medical Leave Act," *Yale Law Journal* 112 (2003): 1943.

who can bring constitutional claims, when those claims are ripe for decision, and what kinds of constitutional claims courts can decide mean that a variety of constitutional issues will rarely, if ever, come before the courts. As relatively passive adjudicators of disputes brought before them by others, the courts also lack the agenda-setting power and resources to undertake widespread investigations of systemic problems. Thus, Sager and Post argued, even if the courts have final say on many constitutional issues, there is considerable room for the political branches to fill in the gaps left by constitutional adjudication.

Indeed, the Fourteenth Amendment, which guarantees equal protection of the laws and due process to all persons in the United States, expressly authorizes Congress "to enforce, by appropriate legislation, the provisions of this article." Thus, the Fourteenth Amendment seems to acknowledge a special role for Congress to play in enforcing at least those rights encompassed within its terms. Congressional enforcement of rights has several advantages over judicial enforcement. Unlike the courts, Congress can set its own agenda and engage in expansive investigations of systemic problems. Its power is not restricted by the justiciability doctrines that limit courts' authority to act. Congress has more information-gathering powers than do the courts, which generally (although not exclusively) must rely on the advocates before them. And because Congress passes laws rather than renders constitutional decisions, it can be more experimental, flexible, and tentative in its actions. Statutes enforcing the Fourteenth Amendment, unlike judicial decisions, are not governed by stare decisis. That flexibility may encourage Congress to try things that the courts would feel reluctant to undertake.

Mark Tushnet took Sager and Post's arguments still further, arguing against judicial supremacy.[13] Where Sager and Post argued for Congressional latitude when Congress has been authorized to act and when the judiciary underenforces constitutional norms, Tushnet's goal

13. Tushnet, *Taking the Constitution Away From the Courts.*

is more radical: to "take the Constitution away from the courts." He disputed the widely accepted notion that the Supreme Court should have final say on constitutional matters and urged a more populist understanding of constitutionalism, in which, at least with respect to certain constitutional rights, the Court is only one player in the constitutional game, lacking final say on what those rights consist of.

One need not go so far as Tushnet. One can acknowledge that there are important reasons for the Court to have final say on constitutional matters while still insisting on the importance of looking beyond the courts as a focal point for progressive constitutional politics. In some instances, the appeal to constitutional values can take a populist form, bypassing the courts altogether. An inspiring example of the latter strategy is the campaign led by the Bill of Rights Defense Committee (BORDC) to get local towns and cities to adopt resolutions condemning the civil liberties abuses of the Patriot Act and the war on terror. This campaign began in Amherst, Massachusetts, shortly after the Patriot Act was signed into law. A small group of people concerned with the threats to civil liberties posed by the Patriot Act, and dismayed by how quickly and easily Congress adopted it, decided to launch a grassroots campaign. The campaign focused on the local level and gave ordinary people an opportunity to take concrete action in defense of their liberties. Although it began in all the usual places—Amherst, Northampton, Berkeley, Santa Monica—by mid-2004, more than 340 towns, cities, and counties had adopted such resolutions, including most of the biggest cities in the country—New York City, Los Angeles, Chicago, Detroit, Philadelphia, San Francisco, even Dallas. Four states—Vermont, Hawaii, Alaska, and Maine—have also adopted such resolutions.

The resolutions don't have much legal force, but they appear to have had remarkable political influence. Since the Patriot Act was enacted, Congress has done little to question it. The executive branch has refused even to disclose how it is using many of the act's most controversial provisions. Only one court has declared any part of the

Patriot Act unconstitutional.[14] Yet the Patriot Act's political valence has changed dramatically. When it was adopted, only one senator—Russ Feingold from Wisconsin—voted against it. Today, many of those who voted for it have expressed reservations and doubts. Several bills have been introduced to amend it. Virtually every Democratic presidential candidate criticized the Patriot Act in their stump speeches, including those who voted for it as senators. A Republican introduced a bill in the House to cut off funding for one controversial provision (authorizing secret searches), and the bill passed by a margin of almost 200 votes. The Bush administration was forced on the defensive. It did not seek to advance most of the provisions of a bill leaked in February 2002 and quickly dubbed "Patriot 2." It also sent John Ashcroft on a national speaking tour to defend the Patriot Act. You don't need to send the Attorney General out to defend a statute that only one senator opposes. Obviously, the tides had turned, and if one looks for the cause of that turn, the BORDC's resolution campaign is the most likely candidate.

In my view, this is an example of popular constitutionalism outside the courts at its very best. The resolution campaign appeals to people's sense of constitutional values of liberty, privacy, checks and balances, and transparency. It bypasses the courts altogether, instead asking local communities to take a stand on what they understand the Constitution to require. Each time a resolution is proposed in a local jurisdiction, it provides an opportunity for public education and debate about constitutional values and their place in the war on terror. Each time a resolution campaign is undertaken, it creates a network of concerned citizens who can be mobilized the next time something like Patriot 2 is pulled out and presented to Congress in response to a terrorist attack.

Although efforts such as these to look beyond the courts for con-

14. *Humanitarian Law Project v. Ashcroft*, 399 F.Supp.2d 1185 (C.D. Cal. 2004).

stitutional norm enforcement are important, they share an inherent problem. Nonjudicial approaches to constitutionalism ultimately rely on majoritarian processes to advance what are often countermajoritarian values. Yet, we have a Constitution that cannot be changed by ordinary legislation precisely because the ordinary political process is often inadequate to protect certain kinds of rights and values. For example, while we understand that, in general, the rights of the criminal process are important for ensuring that innocent people are not convicted and that police power is properly constrained, we also know that, in particular cases, we are likely to be sorely tempted to reject those protections as "technicalities." Similarly, while we understand that a democracy depends on freedom of speech, we also recognize that in times of crisis the majority may be tempted to suppress dissenting voices, as we did most dramatically during World War I and the McCarthy era.

If constitutional values are enshrined in the Constitution because we cannot rely on majoritarian processes to protect them, then a theory of constitutionalism that ultimately relies on those majoritarian processes is inherently problematic. Although political processes may work better to protect some rights than others, especially those rights in which the majority has an immediate interest, such as privacy, they are unlikely to work very well at protecting the rights of dissenters or minorities. Accordingly, while it is absolutely critical that progressives look beyond the courts, in particular to grassroots initiatives and organizing, it is also essential that they do not lightly abandon the notion that courts have special authority and special responsibility to protect the rights of those who cannot protect themselves through the political process.

Looking to the States

Some advocates for progressive social change have suggested that if the federal courts are hostile, litigants should look to state constitutions and courts to advance their claims. The states are bound by the

Constitution's Supremacy Clause to respect a floor of constitutional rights set by Supreme Court doctrine, but they are free to go above that floor by adopting more expansive rights protections than exist at the federal level. On a variety of issues, progressives have adopted this strategy with some success. Although such localized and decentralized strategies are certainly less efficient than a federal victory, looking to the states is an important option when the federal courts have denied relief. In addition to finding more hospitable forums, state and local initiatives may provide opportunities for building a base of committed and engaged citizens around campaigns for social change. Citizens are often more likely to feel that they can make an impact at the local level than at the federal level. As the cliché goes, "all politics is local." Moreover, because state court decisions do not require immediate application to the entire nation, state courts may feel more latitude in experimenting with novel arguments and approaches to common problems.

Progressives have relied on state constitutional litigation to advance social reform and individual rights beyond the U.S. Supreme Court's baseline in two areas in particular—public school finance and criminal justice. Although there are significant success stories in both areas, the state litigation strategy has also proven less of a panacea than some might have hoped.

In the criminal justice area, state courts have interpreted their own state constitutions in ways that afford substantially more protection to citizens in the law-enforcement setting than has the U.S. Supreme Court. State courts have adopted more rights-protective rules in rules governing searches and seizures,[15] police interrogation and confessions,[16] and the right to counsel. On the whole, however, state

15. See generally George Bundy Smith and Janet A. Gordon, "Police Encounters With Citizens and the Fourth Amendment: Similarities and Differences Between Federal and State Law," *Temple Law Review* 68 (1995): 1317.

16. See generally Mary A. Crossley, "Note: *Miranda* and the State Constitution: State Courts Take a Stand," *Vanderbilt Law Review* 39 (1986): 1693.

courts have followed the lead of the Supreme Court on criminal defendants' rights.

The success stories are impressive. For example, several states have declined to follow the Supreme Court in creating various exceptions to the "exclusionary rule," which generally forbids the use of evidence obtained in violation of the Fourth Amendment against a defendant in a criminal case. In 1984, the Supreme Court created a substantial exception to this rule—the "good faith" exception. In *United States v. Leon*,[17] the Court ruled that evidence obtained by officers who reasonably relied on an illegal warrant mistakenly issued by a magistrate is admissible in court, in spite of the constitutional violation. A number of state courts, however, have refused to adopt a similar good faith exception to state constitutional exclusionary rules.[18] For example, in *People v. Bigelow*,[19] the New York Court of Appeals reasoned that an exception to the exclusionary rule would frustrate the rule's purpose by providing an incentive for illegal police conduct.

States have also parted company with the Supreme Court on rules that govern police–citizen encounters. For example, although the Supreme Court has condoned both consent searches and pretext stops, two practices that facilitate racial profiling, state courts have read their own constitutions to be more protective. The Supreme Court's "consent search" doctrine holds that police may approach anyone and request consent to search without any basis for suspicion. In addition, the Court has ruled that police need not inform the individual that he or she has the right to decline consent. The "pretext stop" doctrine permits police to use the pretext of a traffic violation, or indeed any other violation, to justify a stop or arrest, even where the police have no interest in enforcing the law that ostensibly justified the stop and

17. 468 U.S. 897 (1984).
18. 497 N.Y.S.2d 630, 637 (N.Y. 1985).
19. See, for example, *State v. Novembrino*, 519 A.2d 820 (N.J. 1987); *State v. Marsala*, 579 A.2d 58 (Conn. 1990); *State v. Carter*, 370 S.E.2d 553 (N.C. 1988); *State v. Guzman*, 842 P.2d 660 (Idaho 1992).

would not have stopped the individual for that particular infraction if not for some ulterior motive. Because these doctrines essentially permit law-enforcement officers to conduct stops and searches without objective individualized suspicion regarding the offenses they are actually investigating, they effectively permit police to rely on illegitimate criteria, such as race, to decide whom to stop and search.[20]

State courts have been far more skeptical of such tactics. The New Jersey Supreme Court has held that for a consent search to be valid under its state constitution, the police must show not only that the consent was voluntary (which is all the U.S. Supreme Court requires) but also that the individual was aware of his or her right to refuse consent.[21,22] Both New Jersey's and Hawaii's Supreme Courts have ruled that under their constitutions, police must have "reasonable and articulable suspicion" of criminal activity before requesting motorists to consent to a search.[23] Similarly, some state courts have held pretextual arrests impermissible under their own constitutions. For instance, the Arkansas Supreme Court held in *State v. Sullivan* that pretextual arrests—defined as arrests that would not have occurred but for an ulterior investigative motive—are unreasonable as a matter of state constitutional law.[24] The Washington Supreme Court has also rejected the federal rule in deciding pretexual arrest cases under its own constitution.[25] These decisions give individuals broader rights protections than they would otherwise have under federal law and substantially reduce opportunities for racial profiling.

State courts have also been more generous than the U.S. Supreme Court with respect to the right to counsel. The U.S. Supreme Court has held that the Sixth Amendment right to counsel prevents law-

20. See Cole, *No Equal Justice*, 27–41.
21. Ibid.
22. *State v. Johnson*, 346 A.2d 66, 68 (N.J. 1975).
23. *State v. Carty*, 790 A.2d 903 (N.J. 2002); *State v. Kearns*, 867 P.2d 903 (Haw. 1994).
24. *State v. Sullivan*, 74 S.W.3d 215, 220–21 (Ark. 2002).
25. See *State v. Ladson*, 979 P.2d 833 (Wash. 1999).

enforcement officers from deliberately eliciting statements from a suspect in the absence of counsel after he has been indicted or otherwise formally charged.[26] However, it has ruled that there is no Sixth Amendment right to counsel until the suspect has been formally charged, meaning that the right does not apply when an individual is being investigated or even after he has been arrested and taken into custody, as long as he has not yet been charged. Several state courts have disagreed. In *Blue v. State*, the Supreme Court of Alaska held that, under the state constitution, the right to counsel attaches during a preindictment lineup unless exigent circumstances exist such that providing counsel would unduly interfere with a prompt investigation.[27] In so holding, the court found that ensuring the suspect's right to fair procedures outweighed the need for prompt investigation in most circumstances.[28] Other state courts have interpreted their constitutions to extend the right to counsel before indictment in various contexts, such as at the taking of a blood-alcohol test,[29] the giving of a handwriting sample,[30] or the arrest itself.[31]

These examples illustrate that state courts can prove hospitable to rights claims rejected by the U.S. Supreme Court. However, these are isolated examples; most state courts simply follow the U.S. Supreme Court in interpreting their own constitutions on matters of criminal procedure. In addition, these decisions are usually not the result of a coordinated progressive campaign; rather, they reflect the work of individual criminal defense attorneys in individual cases around the country. Although state criminal defense lawyers and public defenders do share strategies and arguments, just as prosecutors do, these deci-

---

26. *Massiah v. United States*, 377 U.S. 201, 206 (1964); *Powell v. Alabama*, 287 U.S. 45 (1932).

27. *Blue v. State*, 558 P.2d 636, 642 (Alaska 1977).

28. Ibid.

29. See *Friedman v. Commissioner of Public Safety*, 473 N.W.2d 828, 835 (Minn.1991); *State v. Welch*, 376 A.2d 351, 355 (1977).

30. See *Roberts v. State*, 458 P.2d 340, 342 (Alaska 1969).

31. See *Commonwealth v. Richman*, 320 A.2d 351, 353 (Pa. 1974).

sions are usually not the result of a coordinated campaign for progressive legal reform.

Unlike criminal defense, there has been a sustained campaign to look to state courts for progressive reform on issues of school funding. Again, the impetus was an inhospitable Supreme Court. In 1973, the U.S. Supreme Court ruled that the Constitution did not guarantee a right to equal educational funding across school districts. In *San Antonio Independent School District v. Rodriguez*,[32] the Court rejected an equal protection challenge to the Texas school funding scheme, which was based largely on local property taxes and which resulted in substantially more public funds per pupil for schools in wealthy districts than for schools in poor districts.

Advocates of educational equity had also filed suits in state courts, arguing that the state constitutions guaranteed more than the federal constitution. The state courts responded much more favorably than had the U.S. Supreme Court. Only thirteen days after *Rodriguez* was decided, for example, the New Jersey Supreme Court struck down its state education financing scheme, finding that it violated the state constitution's guarantee of equality.[33] In 1976, the California Supreme Court followed suit, ruling that California's funding scheme violated the California Constitution's equal protection provisions.[34] Other efforts were less successful, however: state supreme courts decided twenty-one school finance cases between 1973 and 1989, and plaintiffs won only six.

In 1989, the Kentucky Supreme Court shifted the focus of education finance litigation. In *Rose v. Council for Better Education*,[35] the court relied not on equality guarantees in the state constitution but on a provision guaranteeing "an efficient system of common schools." Finding that the state educational system failed to meet this consti-

---

32. 411 U.S. 1 (1973).
33. *Robinson v. Cahill*, 303 A.2d 273 (N.J. 1973).
34. *Serrano v. Priest*, 557 P.2d 929 (Cal. 1976).
35. 790 S.W.2d 186 (Ky. 1989).

tutional requirement for all of its students, the court issued a detailed order specifying seven capacities that the state must provide for each student and nine essential features of an "efficient system of common schools." After the Kentucky decision, supreme courts in several other states similarly found their educational systems inadequate, relying on constitutional guarantees to education rather than on equality provisions. In all, plaintiffs prevailed in twelve of twenty-four state education finance lawsuits between 1989 and 2000.

Victories in the state courts did not always translate into progress on the ground. The difficulty of implementing judicial decrees in the school finance litigation recalls the struggles the Supreme Court and lower federal courts faced in attempting to implement *Brown v. Board of Education*. Obstacles to institutional reform have proven persistent, even where courts have been willing to recognize a constitutional problem and mandate its resolution. New Jersey provides perhaps the best example: since the New Jersey Supreme Court ruled in 1973 that the school finance system violated the state's constitution, the court has issued more than a dozen decisions on education finance. The legislature was initially reluctant to implement the court's decree, and the court was forced first to order the legislature to comply by a set date and then to extend that deadline. The legislature did not act until faced with a court-created "provisional remedy" that would go into effect unless the legislature acted by a specific date. The court initially ruled that the legislative remedy cured the defects identified in the system, but in 1990, the court once again found the system unconstitutional and ordered increased spending in the state's poor districts. In 1994, the court ruled that the legislature's response to its 1990 decision was inadequate, leading to a new legislative overhaul of the system in 1996. The court found the 1996 overhaul insufficient as well and ordered still further remedies. The litigation is ongoing, and New Jersey ranks forty-second in overall equity in an *Education Week* ranking.

As this account suggests, shifting the focus of reform efforts to state courts may not be enough to achieve progressive social reform, even in states with relatively receptive state supreme courts. Obstacles to broad structural change are substantial, no matter what judicial forum one finds oneself in. Structural reform efforts in state and federal judicial forums alike have made it clear that court victories are rare and that even where cases are won, they are usually not enough to achieve real change. Although litigation is important, and often necessary, it is rarely sufficient to resolve systemic social injustices at the state or federal level. Perhaps the most important lesson of the past fifty years is that the progressive lawyer must look beyond the courts altogether.

A Different View of Litigation

Many progressives continue to view federal litigation as playing an important role in struggles for social reform, but they tend to see lawsuits not as the centerpiece of reform efforts but as one part of a larger campaign. Those involved in the day-to-day work of social change have not given up on the courts entirely, but they have learned that successful social change requires a more comprehensive campaign addressed to a variety of forums at the same time. Whereas the NAACP Legal Defense Fund's desegregation strategy was focused on courts, progressives today understand lawsuits as playing a more humble role in the struggle for social change: the lawsuits may provide a focus for organizing and public education, a spur to political reform, or a way of dislodging information that can be used more broadly to pursue reform.

The campaign to end racial profiling provides one example of the modern, multifaceted approach to social reform. More progress has been made on the issue of racial profiling in the past five years than on probably any issue of equity in criminal justice enforcement over the past several decades. Before the mid-1990s, racial profiling was not even a recognized phenomenon outside minority communities. News stories occasionally reported anecdotes involving individual

African Americans who had been repeatedly stopped by the police for minor traffic infractions, but the problem was not understood as systemic. In the mid- to late-1990s, however, that understanding shifted. By the end of the decade, polls reported that 80 percent of Americans considered racial profiling wrong.

By 2004, more than half the state's legislatures had enacted bills addressed to racial profiling. Twenty states prohibited the practice; New Jersey made it a felony. Thirteen states mandated training for police to discourage practices and attitudes that lead to profiling. Seventeen states instituted some sort of reporting requirement. Countless city and local jurisdictions similarly adopted antiprofiling policies. Both President Clinton and President George W. Bush spoke out against racial profiling. President Bush issued a memorandum that generally forbade racial profiling by federal agents, although the memo provided no enforcement mechanism.

Much remains to be done, however. The public consensus on racial profiling was challenged by the terrorist attacks of September 11, 2001, after which polls reported that 60 percent of Americans now favored ethnic profiling of Arabs and Muslims. The Bush administration's policy statement on racial and ethnic profiling forbids it for ordinary law enforcement but permits it for border control and national security purposes. In addition, the Bush administration has, since September 11, embarked on the most massive ethnic profiling campaign seen since foreign nationals and American citizens of Japanese descent were interned during World War II; yet, public outcry has been muted.

The racial profiling reforms that have been achieved are by no means complete solutions. States have not always followed through on the legislative reforms they have adopted, and some of the reforms themselves were fundamentally flawed. Still, compared with other areas of race and criminal justice, where racial disparities have grown increasingly stark without much public protest outside minority communities, the progress made on racial profiling has been remarkable.

The practice of racial profiling undoubtedly raises serious constitutional concerns. It involves the use of racial generalizations as a factor in official state decisions—such as who the police stop, arrest, and search—and, under constitutional equal protection doctrine, any official reliance on race triggers the most stringent judicial scrutiny. Yet the progress described above has been made largely through the political branches rather than through the courts. Lawsuits have, in some instances, played an important role as a catalyst for change. However, the most successful suits have resulted not in rulings that racial profiling was illegal but in settlements that required the police to report on the demographics of their stop-and-search practices. One such settlement, in a suit by Robert Wilkins, a black Harvard Law School graduate who had been stopped unlawfully by Maryland state police, led in 1998 to the first systemic statistical demonstration that blacks and Hispanics were disproportionately stopped and searched.[36] That report led to pressure for similar studies in other states, and the campaign against racial profiling was off and running. A lawsuit in New Jersey played a similar role. And in New York City, Philadelphia, and other jurisdictions, lawsuits arising out of racial profiling incidents led to settlements that required training, reporting, or both. But the bulk of the change has come through the political branches—through state legislatures, local municipalities, and individual police chiefs. In the profiling area, then, cases were sometimes useful as a spur to change, or as a means to obtain information, but actual change almost always came through legislative or executive initiative rather than by court decree.

Why have progressives been able to make more progress on racial profiling than on other areas of inequity in criminal justice? This question underscores the ways in which progressives have rethought strategy in a less hospitable climate. Racial profiling was susceptible to political reform for a variety of reasons. First, the phenomenon

36. Cole, *No Equal Justice*, 34–36.

affects minorities of all classes, and therefore it cannot be dismissed or ignored simply because it affects the most vulnerable among us. Black and Hispanic doctors, athletes, lawyers, and teachers were frequently subjected to racial profiling, and because of their status in the community, their stories were often perceived as more credible and influential than a complaint of a poor young black man from the inner city. Second, racial profiling often manifests itself in a traffic stop, one of the few police–citizen encounters that most Americans have personally experienced. These facts about profiling mean that the issue resonated across a broader spectrum, and progressives were able to use that to their advantage to achieve political support for change.

Third, a key to the progressive strategy on racial profiling was not to ask for too much. By and large, the request for reform took the form of demanding studies. Who can be against studying a problem, particularly after virtually all of the initial studies revealed that the phenomenon was widespread and systemic? The studies' results usually disclosed substantial racial disparities in stop and, especially, search data, which then created pressure for further reform. Indeed, the mere existence of the studies may have had a positive effect on police behavior. The systemic nature of profiling suggests that much of it is based on unconscious or subconscious stereotypes about minority race and crime, stereotypes that are deeply ingrained in American culture. Without clear signals from one's superiors that such stereotypes should play no role in policing, they are almost certain to play a role, as the racial profiling studies suggest. The very fact that a state legislature or city council has mandated a study of profiling sends a message to police that profiling is wrong and that their actions will be monitored; and that message is likely to have some ameliorative effect on the practice of profiling.

Thus, the racial profiling campaign illustrates an understanding of lawsuits as just one small part of a larger campaign for change. Other, more classic examples of using litigation to facilitate political reform include cases seeking to safeguard First Amendment rights to speech and association, which may help keep open the pathways for other progressive political change. Without the opportunities to debate, demonstrate, and organize, political change is virtually impossible. The classic example of this type of litigation comes from the civil rights movement, where lawyers frequently filed First Amendment lawsuits to protect civil rights demonstrators and organizers.[37]

At the same time, progressives have increasingly been put in the position of using constitutional law defensively—not to demand political change but to defend progressive reform that is being attacked by conservatives on constitutional grounds. By necessity, progressives have been heavily involved in litigation over Congress's right to implement equal protection and due process rights under Section 5 of the Fourteenth Amendment, over the rights of state and federal governments to regulate campaign finance in the interest of reducing the distorting effects of concentrated wealth, over the ability of state universities to adopt and carry out affirmative action plans, and over environmental regulations challenged as interfering with property rights. These challenges are often brought by conservative public interest organizations, advocating rights of states, property, or equal protection. Progressives enter the fray to defend the prerogatives of the federal and state political branches to adopt legislation for social change. Here, as in First Amendment litigation, the progressive lawyer argues not that the courts should order social reform but merely that they should keep open other political avenues for social change.

Even where progressive lawyers ask the courts to order change directly, they usually see the lawsuits not as the main engine of reform but as an opportunity to advance political organizing or to galvanize public debate around a particular issue. Progressives have long understood that lawsuits will be successful only if there is substantial polit-

37. See, for example, *NAACP v. Alabama*, 357 U.S. 449 (1958); *Edwards v. South Carolina*, 372 U.S. 229 (1963); *Garner v. Louisiana*, 368 U.S. 157 (1961).

ical support for the causes they advocate. They have therefore sought to fill courtrooms with supporters, organize demonstrations, and run public education campaigns in the hopes of increasing the likelihood of victory in court. In the past, these efforts were seen as secondary, as supplements to the "main event" taking place in the courtroom. Today, however, progressives understand that the political support itself may be the engine of change exercised through channels other than the litigation. Thus, the lawsuit becomes not the focal point of the strategy but an opportunity for organizing, educating, and mobilizing forces for political change. On this theory, even lawsuits that are very likely to be losers in court may serve a progressive's legal agenda.[38]

The recent litigation challenging the detention of "enemy combatants" held at Guantanamo Bay, Cuba, illustrates the point. When lawyers from the Center for Constitutional Rights filed suit in 2002 on behalf of several Guantanamo detainees, most experts considered their chance of success virtually nil. The judicial precedents were dead set against them. The Supreme Court had ruled that foreign nationals who have not entered the United States have no constitutional rights. In World War II, the Court had ruled that the courthouse doors were closed to "enemy aliens" captured and tried abroad by the military for war crimes. Moreover, the Guantanamo clients, described by high-level administration officials as "the worst of the worst," were hardly sympathetic. As the experts predicted, the district court and court of appeals unanimously rejected the detainees' challenge, ruling that the plaintiffs were barred at the door.

However, the lawyers who brought these cases did not merely make arguments in the federal courts. They turned the lawsuits into a dramatic focus for galvanizing political support to the cause of the detainees, who were being held incommunicado and indefinitely with-

38. See Jules Lobel, *Success Without Victory: Lost Legal Battles and the Long Road to Justice in America* (New York: New York University Press, 2003).

out any sort of hearing whatsoever. Because the detainees were all foreign nationals, the lawyers focused much of their attention on international opinion. In Great Britain in particular, the cases became a cause célèbre and a political thorn in the side of the Tony Blair government. Political objections to Guantanamo were not limited to Great Britain; rather, they extended around the world. The United States came under increasingly harsh international criticism for its claim—in defending the lawsuit—that it had unchecked unilateral authority to hold the detainees forever without any legal limitations.

The international opprobrium occasioned by Guantanamo likely played a significant role in the Supreme Court's surprise decision to agree to review the case. The Court rarely accepts review of cases in which there is no conflict in the lower courts, and even more rarely where the federal government has won. Yet to almost everyone's surprise, the Court did grant review. The mere fact that the Court granted review, and thus posed the real possibility that the executive's authority might actually be subject to legal oversight and limitation, led the administration to adopt a range of ameliorative steps even before the Supreme Court ruled. It released the juveniles (some as young as 13 years old) who had been held in Guantanamo. It released many others, including two British detainees on whose behalf one of the Guantanamo cases had been filed. For the first time, it explained to the public and the world the internal processes it had employed to decide whom to incarcerate at Guantanamo Bay. It also instituted annual parole-type review procedures to assess whether detainees could be released. In the end, the Guantanamo detainees won in the Supreme Court, as the Court rejected the administration's position of unchecked power and ruled that the detainees could file challenges to the legality of their detentions in federal court. Even if the Guantanamo litigants had lost in the Supreme Court, however, the lawsuit was successful in galvanizing the international and domestic pressure that brought about significant change even *before* the Supreme Court had ruled.

The Guantanamo case was ultimately successful. But the more important point is that even before it succeeded in the courts, the case had served to galvanize public and world opinion around the issue of the indefinite detentions of foreign nationals at Guantanamo. Increasingly, progressives view lawsuits not so much for the direct results they might obtain from a judicial decree but from the vantage point of how the suits might contribute to a more comprehensive political/legal campaign. The Guantanamo detentions and racial profiling are two of the more prominent examples that illustrate a much broader theme in progressive law reform today—a theme that sees a much more humble role for courts and that demands a broader strategy for social change.

Looking Outward

The Guantanamo litigation also exemplifies a more novel strategic development in progressive reform movements, namely, looking outward to create pressure for change within. As noted above, much of the political pressure generated by the Guantanamo campaign came from abroad. Nothing more dramatically illustrated this than the fact that 176 members of Great Britain's Parliament filed an amicus brief in the Supreme Court on behalf of the Guantanamo detainees. Prime Minister Blair was compelled by the political pressure within Great Britain to advocate on behalf of the Britons held at Guantanamo, and President Bush was ultimately forced to agree to send several British detainees back to England, where they were promptly released.

The Guantanamo issue was particularly susceptible to international pressure, of course, because the detainees came from forty-two different countries and because the United States needs the cooperation of many of those countries if it is going to protect itself against al Qaeda and other potential enemies. In the age of globalization, progressive lawyers are increasingly realizing that the international arena might be an important part of the strategy for achieving social reform at home.

This shift in focus has substantive as well as strategic implications. Progressive lawyers increasingly cite international human rights norms in U.S. courts. The Guantanamo plaintiffs, for example, claimed that their indefinite incommunicado detention without a hearing violated not only due process but also the Geneva Conventions and the customary law of war. In *Turkmen v. Ashcroft*, a class action lawsuit filed by the Center for Constitutional Rights challenging the treatment of Arab and Muslim foreign nationals detained on immigration charges in connection with the investigation of the September 11 attacks, plaintiffs alleged not only constitutional claims but also violations of international human rights norms. Another lawsuit, *Arar v. Ashcroft*, arising from the U.S. deportation of a Canadian to Syria, where he was tortured and imprisoned for ten months without charges, also directly alleged violations of international human rights norms.

Lawyers also increasingly cite both international human rights norms and other nation's constitutional law decisions as a guide to the interpretation of U.S. law. In *Lawrence v. Texas*,[39] the Supreme Court in 2003 invalidated a Texas statute criminalizing homosexual sodomy on due process grounds, reversing its own precedent to the contrary from seventeen years earlier. In doing so, the Court cited a decision from the European Court of Human Rights similarly invalidating a criminal sodomy statute. If norms of due process are evolving, the way that other courts have resolved similar questions may inform the content of due process under our Constitution. Similarly, when critics have challenged the constitutionality of imposing the death penalty on juveniles and the mentally retarded, they have relied on international human rights norms and a comparative analysis of other nations sharing liberal democratic traditions to argue that inflicting the death penalty in these situations is cruel and unusual. It is not uncommon for courts of other nations to look to American and other nation's precedents as they confront questions under their

---

39. 123 S. Ct. 2476 (2003).

own constitutions; it is becoming less uncommon for our courts to reciprocate. Where other countries or the international human rights legal paradigm have advanced beyond American constitutional law in progressive directions, international human rights and comparative constitutional law are important tools in the progressive lawyer's arsenal.

The international human rights framework also has implications for the tactics employed by domestic progressive campaigns. International human rights groups such as Amnesty International and Human Rights Watch have typically relied much more heavily on public education and "shaming" than on filing lawsuits to advance their causes. In part, this is a matter of necessity. Domestic courts in countries with abusive human rights practices are often deeply compromised, and, with the exception of the European Court of Human Rights, international forums typically lack the power to make their judgments stick. But while human rights groups have typically employed the "reporting" approach against other nations, they are now increasingly employing it against the United States as well.

Issuing reports on human rights abuses in the United States can be a powerful tool for social reform. The United States has long sought to export democracy, human rights, and the rule of law, so it is particularly susceptible to criticism when it fails to live up to the standards it has sought to impose on others. Especially since the terrorist attacks of September 11, the United States is increasingly viewed around the world as ignoring international law and basic human rights, and that perception is undermining the U.S. standing in ways that are difficult to ignore. As a result, international shame may be a particularly powerful force for influencing change within the United States. This is especially true with respect to our treatment of foreign nationals, as other nations have a direct stake in monitoring and pressuring the United States with regard to the treatment of their citizens.

Conclusion

The heyday of progressive law reform has been over for nearly two generations. Progressives today face an inhospitable climate wherever they turn—Congress, the executive, and the federal courts. This reality has forced progressives to hone their arguments and adapt their strategies. In the end, however, progressivism may well be stronger for this adversity. Progressives have moderated their demands for substantive equality, not only because they face hostile forums but also because efforts to achieve equality over the past half century have revealed that the problem is more nuanced than we might have once thought—and requires more nuanced solutions. Claims of affirmative rights and substantive equality have given way to arguments that rights ought to be defined in such a way as not to exploit the vulnerable. Progressives have learned to supplement moral claims with more utilitarian and pragmatic contentions, arguing that respect for rights of the vulnerable, in fact, serves the interest of the majority in a variety of concrete ways.

At the same time, progressives have had to alter their tactics as they seek progressive reform through law. They have looked outside the courts altogether; sought more favorable forums in state courts; reconceived lawsuits as part of a larger, more comprehensive strategy for reform; and most recently, invoked international norms to increase pressure for change at home. Each of these strategies was adopted out of necessity, when it became clear that federal court litigation in and of itself was no longer (if it ever was) the answer. But these adaptations have made progressivism stronger, both in terms of the appeals it makes to the public at large and in terms of its ability to bring about change. For the moment, it means that progressives are not left empty-handed, despite facing difficult odds. And in the future, when the political tide turns back to a climate more friendly to progressive ideals, as it surely will, this experience of adversity will only make progressivism more effective in its effort to produce a more just and equitable world.

CHAPTER SIX

The Poverty of Progressivism and the Tragedy of Civil Society

Jeffrey C. Isaac

THE UNCERTAIN FATE of progressivism in America has been a recurrent theme of public intellectual contention for well over a century. In that time, American politics has experienced recurrent waves of discontent, reform, and stasis. The reforms of the progressive era, the New Deal, and the Great Society can be thought of in terms of such cycles. That the United States has recently been experiencing a prolonged stasis is a diagnosis shared by many commentators and articulated cogently in E. J. Dionne Jr.'s acclaimed book on the subject— *Why Americans Hate Politics*—a book that, though over a decade old, is still frequently cited as having captured an enduring truth about our contemporary political life. Stasis, impasse, interregnum—for a variety of reasons, we are deeply disposed to believe that such conditions ought not to persist and cannot persist, that difficulties should and will be resolved in the course of time. Thus, Dionne's diagnosis has given rise among many liberals to the notion that a progressive revival is in the cards. Following Walter Lippmann's influential pro-

This chapter draws on Isaac, *The Poverty of Progressivism: The Future of American Democracy in a Time of Liberal Decline* (Lanham, MD: Rowman & Littlefield, 2003).

gressive era essay "Drift and Mastery," these progressive liberals discern drift, and they seek, and anticipate, a new form of mastery.

The idea that American society is currently poised for another wave of progressive reform has had remarkable staying power for well over a decade. Originally buoyed by the promise attributed to the Clinton victory in 1992, this idea has persisted in the face of the disappointing domestic record of the Clinton administration, the ignominious 2000 defeat of Gore, the illiberal consequences of the war on terror undertaken by the Bush administration in response to the September 2001 terrorist attacks, and, indeed, in the face of George W. Bush's continued popularity as a "war president" (of course, this popularity is currently in doubt). The staying power of this idea is a sign of its aspirational and motivational power. And yet, the notion of a new progressive hegemony does not seriously reckon with the profound obstacles confronting such a hegemony. Although American society today may confront pressing challenges analogous to those of a century ago, the social and political structures of opportunity, and indeed the consequences of the long-term exhaustion and delegitimization of progressive liberalism, make a progressive hegemony highly unlikely.

Here I briefly discuss this idea of progressive hegemony and especially its most recent articulations; argue that the notion of such a hegemony is wishful thinking, especially in the wake of September 11; and then consider whether a more modest conception of "new citizenship," rooted in civil society, represents a plausible residue of this conception. I argue that such a politics is plausible, and indeed necessary, but that it is profoundly unsatisfactory. My basic point is that the stasis currently afflicting American politics is likely to persist, and progressive liberals must come to terms with it. Although this is not a heartening perspective that does not lend itself to new activist prescriptions, it seems warranted by the current situation.

A Progressive Revival?

The 1990s saw the emergence of a distinctive set of arguments about the need for a progressive revival. Just as the America of the 1890s was poised before a new century, so, it has been argued, are we, poised at the dawn of a new century, confronting new technological opportunities and severe social challenges that demand a new spirit of progressive reform. Overwhelmed by our own interdependencies, we need new forms of social intelligence. Debilitated by an inflationary rights revolution, we need a more pragmatic, yet vigorous, approach to governmental regulation. Beset by fragmentation and division, we need a new activist public policy, centered around the problems of a postindustrial economy and the decline of middle-class living standards. This policy might repair the social fabric and restore direction and coherence to national life. We must do all this, neoprogressive writers and activists argue, because the only alternative is to submit to the forces of reaction, to squander the prospects for progress presented by new opportunities, and to resign our politics to a prolonged period of suffering, resentment, and antagonism.

John Judis and Michael Lind's 1995 manifesto in the *New Republic*, "For a New American Nationalism," helped bring this broader argument to the foreground of discussion. Criticizing the incoherence of the Clinton administration and the "primitive anti-statism" of Gingrichite republicanism, Judis and Lind called for a new nationalism, inspired by the examples of Alexander Hamilton, Abraham Lincoln, and Theodore Roosevelt and summed up in Herbert Croly's influential *The Promise of American Life* (1909).

> America today faces a situation roughly analogous to the one Roosevelt and the progressives faced. Workers are not threatening to man the barricades against capitalists, but society is divided into mutually hostile camps. . . . [T]he goal of a new nationalism today is to forestall these looming divisions in American society. . . . Can we meet these challenges? In the decades between Lincoln and

Theodore Roosevelt, the country floundered as badly as it has during the last few decades. Their mountebanks were no different from ours; their corruption was even more pervasive; and their sense of political paralysis even more profound. Still, they were able to think and act anew. As we prepare to enter the next century, we believe that we are on the verge of a similar era of national renewal."[1]

This theme was echoed in Dionne's much-cited book *They Only Look Dead*, the subtitle of which aptly sums up its argument: *Why Progressives Will Dominate the Next Political Era.* Opening with an epigraph from Theodore Roosevelt, Dionne endorsed a new progressivism, inspired by Croly, whose "task is to restore the legitimacy of public life by renewing the effectiveness of government and reforming the workings of politics."[2] Similar sentiments were sounded by Jacob Weisberg in *In Defense of Government.* Reviving liberalism, he wrote

> is not a matter of starting from scratch but rather of recovering and renewing lost principles. . . . In its original incarnation, progressivism offers a needed corrective to liberalism as it has come to be defined by the Democratic Party over the past few decades. Looking back to the old Progressives, we find a liberalism without a century's accretion of bad habits, without mawkishness or excess. We find a practical, democratic approach to bettering the country. By reviving progressive ideas, liberals can fit themselves for governing again. By resurrecting the term, we can indicate a break with our recent past and our link to an older tradition.[3]

Similar prescriptions were also developed in Theda Skocpol and Stanley Greenberg's *The New Majority: Toward a Popular Progressive Pol-*

1. John B. Judis and Michael Lind, "For a New American Nationalism," *New Republic* (March 27, 1995), 27.

2. E. J. Dionne Jr., *They Only Look Dead: Why Progressives Will Dominate the Next Political Era* (New York: Simon and Shuster, 1996), 16.

3. Jacob Weisberg, *In Defense of Government: The Fall and Rise of Public Trust* (New York: Scribner's, 1996), 158. See also Michael Tomasky, *Left for Dead: The Life, Death and Possible Resurrection of Progressive Politics in America* (New York: Free Press, 1996).

itics, which maintained that the current moment represents "a period of opportunity for progressives," and that although the tactical strength of liberalism is minimal, the larger unfolding social changes offer political openings for the revival of progressive liberalism.[4]

Perhaps the most ambitious of these calls for a revival of progressivism was Michael Lind's *The Next American Nation*, which proposed that we currently stand poised for economic and cultural renewal at the dawn of a "Fourth American Revolution." Lind outlined an elaborate set of policies designed to turn back the deterioration in middle-class living standards and to cement a strong reformist political coalition. Such policies, he averred, can only succeed as part of a "war on oligarchy" that seeks to make the accumulation of private wealth compatible with overall national interests.[5]

This neoprogressive discourse, though chastened by political events of the past decade, which can hardly be seen as proof of a new progressive ascendancy, has not been dampened. Thus, Bush's presidential victory was interpreted as an anomaly, a sign of the underlying strength of progressive forces (Gore won a popular majority; demographic trends favor Democrats, etc.). Thus, even the war on terrorism undertaken in response to the September 11 attacks was interpreted as a sign of the necessity of progressive politics (the war requires a vigorous governmental response; the anthrax scare highlighted the importance of public health policies; domestic security requires a new attention to public goods and infrastructure [airports, ports, railways, etc.]).

This optimism about the long-term prospects for progressivism is mirrored in three recent books that update, but do not substantially amend, the neoprogressive arguments of the 1990s: John Judis and Ruy Teixeira's *The Emerging Democratic Majority*, Stanley B. Green-

---

4. Stanley B. Greenberg and Theda Skocpol, *The New Majority: Toward a Popular Progressive Politics* (New Haven, CT: Yale University Press, 1997).

5. Michael Lind, *The Next American Nation: The New Nationalism and the Fourth American Revolution* (New York: Free Press, 1995), 301–2.

berg's *The Two Americas: Our Current Political Deadlock and How to Break It*, and Ted Halstead and Michael Lind's *The Radical Center: The Future of American Politics.* In different ways, each book argues that the demographics and economics of American society are inconsistent with the current stasis and that these forces point toward a new progressive hegemony. The first two books, which focus on electoral dynamics, argue that democratic advantages among middle-class professionals, minorities, women, and workers can be the basis for "an emerging Democratic majority." The latter book, which focuses on the functional requirements of a postindustrial, information-based economy, argues that a "new social contract" is necessary for social forces to be liberated from old structures and to function efficiently. None of these books treats these developments as inevitable. All recognize that such developments will require political agencies and strategies. Greenberg was the most explicit in acknowledging the power of the current stasis, which he described as a "game" that offers incentives to both parties to continue working at the margins in the hope of the next electoral victory. Yet none of these books deals, with any degree of seriousness, with the kinds of social movements and political coalitions that might make possible a new hegemony and with the kinds of obstacles that such movements and coalitions confront.

I believe that these neoprogressive visions rest on specious analogies with the past and on weak functionalist arguments. As for the first, although progressivism was a political project of what James Scott called "high modernism," American society is characterized by many postmodern features—most notably a "post-Fordist" economy characterized by extreme forms of flexibility and mobility that defy regulatory mechanisms and that severely test the capacities of the nation-state; new forms of consumerism and consumer credit that severely weaken the "organic solidarities" that in the past grounded oppositional social and political movements; and especially new forms of communication associated with the mass media and with new informational technologies that profoundly call into question the pro-

gressive assumption of any kind of rational public or meaningful public discourse about public problems and their solution. Whereas
previous waves of progressive reform were driven by politically organized social movements, American society today lacks any functional
equivalents of these movements. As for the second book, the existence
of social problems associated with new demographic and economic
structures, and the functional need for these problems to be solved
for society to function more smoothly and fairly, does not necessitate
political agencies capable of addressing these problems in serious ways,
nor does it mean that these problems are likely to be solved. In a
similar vein, the existence of a "demand side" for progressive platforms
and policies does not entail the likelihood of a "supply side" capable
of satisfying this demand for a sustained period. My basic point, then,
is that progressive aspirations are not likely to be realized and that
liberals who subscribe to core progressive values need to think in more
chastened and pragmatic ways about what is possible under current
conditions.

In what follows, I suggest that it is on the terrain of civil society
and its voluntary initiatives and third-sector organizations, and not
on the terrain of the national state and its regulatory agencies, that
the best chance for the advancement of such generally progressive
values as social justice and civic empowerment lies. This does not
mean that civil society and the state can simplistically be counterposed
or that civil society initiatives can succeed without political support
of various kinds. Civil society is surely no panacea, the enthusiasm of
some of its partisans notwithstanding. It simply means that an ambitious agenda of political reform and socioeconomic regulation is
unlikely to be enacted; thus, more modest and localized efforts represent the best hope for a left-liberal politics of democratic problem
solving and public regulation. Theorists of "the new citizenship" and
of the so-called "third way" have correctly seen this. The third way
represents a formula for electoral success, but, more important, it
represents a modest politics that embraces the terms of political real-

ism and conducts itself on the terrain of political retrenchment. Third-way politics, and the civil society–centered initiatives it promotes, has much to recommend itself under current historical conditions. But it is also a profoundly limited and unsatisfying form of politics. Partisans of the third way too rarely acknowledge these limits, thus falling victim to their own form of Panglossian optimism. Instead, I argue, what is called for is an honest acknowledgment of the obstacles and tragic binds confronting left-liberal politics today, as well as a sober commitment to nourishing those efforts that promise, in limited ways to be sure, a modicum of justice and empowerment in the face of these obstacles.

How Civil Society Initiatives Offer an Alternative Means of Advancing Progressive Values

In recent years, an eclectic group of writers and activists from across the political spectrum have turned toward civil society as the answer to today's social problems. Refusing simply to celebrate the retrenchment of political agency in the face of market forces, most civil society advocates acknowledge that serious social problems exist and that meaningful forms of collective response are both necessary and possible. Unlike neoprogressives, however, they maintain that such responses are best located in the sphere of civil society rather than in the sphere of conventional politics and public policy formation. Although there is no simple consensus among them, civil society is typically taken to denote that intermediate sphere between the state and the market, between the modalities of sovereign political decision making and individual self-interest. Some civil society advocates, with roots in conservative and neoconservative critiques of the welfare state and its therapeutic culture, focus on such "moral" institutions as the family and religious congregations.[6] Others, closer to the Left, are

6. See Don E. Eberly, *America's Promise: Civil Society and the Renewal of American Culture* (Lanham, MD: Rowman & Littlefield, 1998), and the Council on Civil

primarily concerned with the injustices of capitalist markets and focus on a broader range of voluntary associations, from nonprofit organizations to community-development corporations to trade unions and social movements.[7] There is no single civil society perspective because one of the premises of the civil society discourse is the plurality of civil society associations and the inadequacy of political programs to express or represent this plurality. There is, nonetheless, a general proposition common to those interested in the revival of civil society: neither the progressive, regulatory state nor the free market is sufficient to address America's social ills, and the only way to address those ills is by strengthening the mediating institutions of society.

As their proponents argue, civil society initiatives and organizations have much to recommend them.

(1) They work on the principle of subsidiarity, typically proposing to solve social problems at the lowest and most proximate level consistent with their solution. They are thus appealing to all those, Right and Left, who are wary of the centralized, bureaucratic state and who seek to promote greater civic engagement through more localized and accessible forms of citizen participation.

(2) They purport to promote civic responsibility, requiring individual citizens to work collaboratively to achieve public goods. In this regard, civil society initiatives can be seen as fostering empowerment rather than dependence, deliberation rather than zero-sum strategic bargaining, and communitarian dispositions rather than predatory practices aimed at colonizing public power on behalf of particular interests.

(3) They purport to rest on social self-organization and on diverse forms of volunteerism. Thus, they do not require large amounts of money to be allocated by the federal government.

Society, *A Call to Civil Society: Why Democracy Needs Moral Truths* (New York: Institute for American Values, 1998).

7. See Benjamin R. Barber, *A Place for Us: How to Make Society Civil and Democracy Strong* (New York: Hill and Wang, 1998).

Civil society initiatives thus combine, at least ideal-typically, the virtues of entrepreneurial effort, efficiency, voluntarism, and civic-mindedness. For this reason, they are often presented as being practical in a way that welfare state regulations and allocations are not. Further, they are often seen as sources of social capital that build trust and confidence in social and political institutions.[8] As Benjamin Barber summed up this view:

> [It] posits a third domain of civic engagement which is neither governmental nor strictly private yet shares the virtues of both. It offers a space for public work, civic business, and other common activities that are focused neither on profit nor on a welfare bureaucracy's client services. It is also a communicative domain of civility, where political discourse is grounded in mutual respect and the search for common understanding even as it expresses differences and identity conflicts. It extols voluntarism but insists that voluntarism is the first step to citizenship, not just an exercise in private character building, philanthropy, or noblesse oblige.[9]

The civil society idea, which has assumed great prominence in contemporary American political discourse, has generated a proliferation of practical experiments that have been promoted by an extensive and increasingly dense network of philanthropic foundations and academic institutions, including the Kettering Foundation, the Pew Charitable Trusts, the Bradley Foundation, the Open Society Institute, the National Civic League, the Hubert Humphrey Center at the University of Minnesota, and the Walt Whitman Center at Rutgers University. Carmen Sirianni and Lewis Friedland, in their book *Civic Innovation in America*, have gone so far as to call this collection of efforts a genuine "movement for civic renewal."

8. See Robert Putnam, *Bowling Alone: The Collapse and Revival of American Community* (New York: Simon and Schuster, 2000); and Richard A. Couto, with Catherine S. Guthrie, *Making Democracy Work Better: Mediating Structures, Social Capital, and the Democratic Prospect* (Chapel Hill: University of North Carolina Press, 1999).

9. Barber, *A Place for Us.*

The promotion of civic renewal initiatives is of great value, and civil society advocates working in this vein have made it clear that even though progressive politics at the level of the national state may be stalled, when one examines the landscape of American society more carefully, one will discover a vigorous civil society politics. As Harry Boyte and Nancy Kari put it, "For all our problems and fears as a nation, civic energy abounds. Americans are not uncaring or apathetic about public affairs. In fact, a rich array of civic work in many diverse settings is evident across the country."[10] Partly in response to the practical limitations of progressive social policy, partly in response to the ideological disrepute of ambitious progressive policy visions, and partly for pragmatic reasons, citizens and civic groups have developed important, innovative practices worth taking very seriously as forms of democratic practice for a post-progressive age. Some examples follow.

Labor

Many neoprogressives note that the dramatic decline of the American labor movement has had harmful distributional and civic consequences, eroding the principal means of working-class social capital, and thereby exacerbating economic inequality.[11] In the face of the manifest political weakness of the organized labor movement, labor activists, working in conjunction with the AFL-CIO and with forward-looking union leaders, have pioneered such innovative efforts as cross-border solidarity networks, campaigns against child labor and sweatshop labor, student efforts to support living wage arrangements

10. Harry C. Boyte and Nancy N. Kari, *Building America: The Democratic Promise of Public Work* (Philadelphia: Temple University Press, 1996), 5.

11. See Ruy Teixeira and Joel Rogers, *America's Forgotten Majority: Why the White Working Class Still Matters* (New York: Basic Books, 2000); Theda Skocpol, *The Missing Middle: Working Families and the Future of American Social Policy* (New York: W. W. Norton, 2000); and Edward N. Wolff, *Top Heavy: The Increasing Inequality of Wealth in America and What Can Be Done About It* (New York: New Press, 1995).

on university campuses, Jobs With Justice efforts to support living wage ordinances, and community tribunals to hear worker grievances and to publicize employer maltreatment of workers. Such efforts—notably the living wage movement—sometimes seek to influence public policy, typically at the local rather than the national level.[12] Sometimes, as in the widely publicized demonstrations against the World Trade Organization in Seattle, Washington, D.C., and Los Angeles, they seek to protest national public policy. More often, they seek to press specific grievances and to influence public opinion, thus shifting public discourse and building solidarity for workers without substantially altering the balance of power between classes or effecting dramatic changes in public policy.[13]

For example, Randy Shaw documented how human rights, labor, and religious activists joined together to pressure Nike to reform its overseas labor practices, which sanctioned repressive and abusive labor relations and extremely low wages in Third World countries, indirectly generating a worldwide race to the bottom regarding wages and working conditions for garment workers.[14] The campaign's outcome was neither a collective bargaining agreement nor a piece of national legislation but simply a "voluntary accord" between Nike and its critics, brokered by the Clinton administration, that required Nike to voluntarily limit its overseas abuses, to pay so-called prevailing wages, and to submit to voluntary forms of quasi-independent monitoring of its labor practices. This accord also led to the formation of a cor-

12. See Robert Pollin, "Living Wage, Live Action," *Nation*, November 23, 1998: 15–20.

13. For a useful overview of many of these efforts that is also a brief on their behalf, see Naomi Klein, *No Logo: Taking Aim at the Brand Bullies* (New York: Picador, 1999). See also Klein, "Does Protest Need a Vision?" *Nation*, 2000; and Martin Hart-Landsberg, "After Seattle: Strategic Thinking About Movement Building," *Monthly Review*, July–August 2000: 112.

14. See Randy Shaw, *Reclaiming America: Nike, Clean Air, and the New National Activism* (Berkeley: University of California Press, 1999), especially 1–96.

poratist organization, the Apparel Industry Partnership (AIP), intended to encourage other apparel manufacturers to undertake similar measures. Subsequent to these developments, the AIP spawned another organization, the Fair Labor Association (FLA), designed to bring together corporations, labor rights groups, and universities behind a program to limit sweatshop abuses. In response to the corporate biases of the FLA, student activists associated with United Students Against Sweatshops, working in tandem with the AFL-CIO, UNITE, and other worker organizations, formed the Workers' Right Consortium (WRC) as an alternative to the corporatist FLA to pursue strategies of independent corporate monitoring. The WRC has pressed almost 100 American universities to affiliate with it.

Significant momentum against sweatshop labor has been generated by these campaigns. In many ways, the effects of such activity have been limited, and it is clear that such campaigns cannot bring the force of law to bear against corporate abuse. As critics point out, prevailing wages in most Third World countries are abominably low, and labor law in these countries affords few rights to workers. Voluntary accords, such as the one brokered with Nike, do very little to alter such harsh realities. They similarly do little, in broad terms, to affect global wage rates or to put an end to the tendency of global sweatshop conditions to depress the wages of American workers. Nonetheless, they can effect some measure of change in those particular factories that become the focus of public attention. Through this, they may create small ripple effects of change. In addition, these accords help raise public awareness about labor issues and express solidarity with poorly treated workers here and abroad.[15] Such efforts are not the result of mass movement activity; they do not substantially enhance the bargaining or political power of organized labor, neither

15. See Archon Fung, Dara O'Rourke, and Charles Sabel, "Realizing Labor Standards: How Transparency, Competition, and Sanctions Could Improve Working Conditions Worldwide," *Boston Review*, February/March 2001: 4–10, 20.

in Third World countries nor in the United States; and they do not add up to a large-scale public policy agenda. Nonetheless, they do have important, if limited, effects on economic life and on the process of political empowerment itself.[16]

The Environment

In the face of declining political support and federal funding for vigorous environmental regulation, new civil society approaches have emerged to supplement, and sometimes replace, top-down bureaucratic regulation of corporations: new forms of deliberation about hazardous waste disposal and appropriate risk that include business, local government, environmental activists and civic associations; public information campaigns about toxic substances, such as the Right to Know Network and Citizens' Clearinghouse on Toxic Waste; civic monitoring of pollution and waste disposal; local green space ordinances, community land trusts and environmental stewardship, and good neighbor agreements. What has come to be called "civic environmentalism" comprises a repertoire of innovative forms of partnership designed to allow local, place-based communities to develop modes of consensus, or at least levels of mutual understanding and trust, about questions of acceptable risk, the costs and benefits of different kinds of toxic cleanups, trade-offs between jobs and the environment, and the most appropriate methods of managing forests, watersheds, and other environmentally sensitive areas.[17] These techniques are partly a response to declining federal ability and inclination to impose environmental solutions.[18] But they are also the result of a

16. See Jeffrey Isaac, "Thinking About the Antisweatshop Movement." *Dissent*, Fall 2001: 36–44.

17. See Bruce A. Williams and Albert R. Matheny, *Democracy, Dialogue, and Environmental Disputes* (New Haven, CT: Yale University Press, 1995); and Andrew Szasz, *Ecopopulism: Toxic Waste and the Movement for Environmental Justice* (Minneapolis: University of Minnesota Press, 1994).

18. See, for example, Katharine Q. Seelye, "Bush Proposing to Shift Burden of Toxic Cleanups to Taxpayers." *New York Times*, February 24, 2002: A1.

learning process that has taught many environmental activists that there are no cost-free ways to make environmental decisions and that bureaucratic regulation is often inferior to consensus building and civic responsibility. In *Civic Innovation in America*, Sirianni and Friedland present an impressive inventory of such efforts, which have sprung up across the country and have worked, in fairly mundane and unpublicized ways, to collaboratively resolve environmental problems at the local level. The results of such innovations are varied, and, unsurprisingly given their modus operandi, such results tend to be localized. But they are not without effect upon environmental policy and local politics.[19] Indeed, civic environmentalism has moved beyond collaborative approaches to the environment to address broader issues related to urban sprawl, "local self-reliance," and "sustainable development." Communities across the United States have thus taken up the theme of civic responsibility to support new modes of land use regulation and regional planning that promote urban density and "compact urban form," neighborhood preservation, environmentally sustainable agriculture, and locally owned business.[20]

Urban Issues

In the absence of a massive federal effort to revitalize impoverished inner cities through public housing subsidy and construction, job cre-

19. Carmen Sirianni and Lewis Friedland, *Civic Innovation in America: Community, Empowerment, Public Policy, and the Movement for Civic Renewal* (Berkeley: University of California Press, 2001), 85–137.

20. See Michael Shuman, *Going Local: Creating Self-Reliant Communities in a Global Age* (New York: Free Press, 1998); Andres Duany, Elizabeth Plater-Zyberk, and Jeff Speck, *Suburban Nation: The Rise of Sprawl and the Decline of the American Dream* (New York: North Point Press, 2000); Myron Orfield, *Metropolitics: A Regional Agenda for Community and Stability* (Washington, DC: Brookings Institution, 1997); and Manuel Pastor Jr., Peter Dreier, J. Eugene Grigsby III, and Marta Lopez-Garza, *Regions That Work: How Cities and Suburbs Can Grow Together* (Minneapolis: University of Minnesota Press, 2000). Michael Sandel discussed such efforts in *Democracy's Discontent* (Cambridge, MA: Harvard University Press, 1996), 334–36.

ation, and the serious enhancement of public education, a range of less ambitious and ad hoc efforts to address urban problems have sprung up throughout the United States: local nonprofit social service agencies that offer child care, support for the victims of domestic abuse, temporary shelter, and job training; community development corporations that seek to leverage public, private, and philanthropic funds to revitalize neighborhoods through the construction of low-cost housing, the establishment of neighborhood-based health clinics and cooperatives, and the promotion of neighborhood-based retail outlets, banks, shopping centers, and other businesses; community development banks that bridge major financial institutions and inner-city communities, countering the effects of redlining and making funds available for community development; community organizations facilitated by the Industrial Areas Foundation, such as East Brooklyn Congregations, which pioneered the Nehemiah Project of building low-cost housing, and Communities Organized for Public Service, which has organized in support of a range of redevelopment efforts in San Antonio; and innovative, locally oriented, third-sector programs designed to build human and social capital, such as YouthBuild and the Algebra Project.[21] According to one of the most articulate advocates of such civil society efforts, they have generated "a surprising legacy of hope as Americans of good spirit have stepped in to do a job that needed to be done. . . . [W]e can look to these small-scale, local efforts to find responses to the problems of poverty

21. For an overview of such initiatives, see Lisbeth Schorr, *Common Purpose: Strengthening Families and Neighborhoods to Rebuild America* (New York: Anchor Books, 1997); Ronald F. Ferguson and William T. Dickens, eds., *Urban Problems and Community Development* (Washington, DC: Brooking Institution, 1997); and Sirianni and Friedland, *Civic Innovation*, 35–84. On the Industrial Areas Foundation, see Sirianni and Friedland, *Civic Innovation*, 43–56; and Harry Boyte, *Commonwealth: A Return to Citizen Politics* (New York: Free Press, 1989), 81–126. On the Algebra Project, see Jeffrey Isaac, "The Calculus of Consent: The Algebra Project and Democratic Politics," *Dissent*, 1998.

that are not only more effective but more humane than our current social service and welfare programs."[22]

Why Civil Society Initiatives Do *Not* Offer an Alternative to Progressivism

The aforementioned efforts clearly hold promise as examples of the way ordinary citizens and grassroots civic organizations can effect a measure of change through their own means. Our sensationalist and media-saturated culture obscures this in its reduction of politics to celebrity gossip, electoral horseraces, and professional punditry. For this reason, civil society efforts are important not only for their practical value but also for their exemplary or symbolic value, as instances of "civic virtue" and dedicated "public work" that should be emulated and extended.

Nonetheless, there are dangers to exaggerating the significance of these efforts because they are typically patently inadequate to the problems they address. Although new labor networks and antisweat campaigns may furnish valuable support and solidarity to workers struggling against the ill effects of untrammeled free trade and financial globalization, such networks have little effect on the ability of workers in the United States or elsewhere to collectively bargain about wages or about working conditions, job security, and the long-term effects of investment decisions. They have just as little effect on the possibilities of national policies regarding employment, trade, or long-term, sustainable development. Such efforts are thus no substitute for a coherent political agenda centered on the concerns of workers and their families.[23]

Similarly, civic environmentalism can help citizens negotiate the

22. Robin Garr, *Reinvesting in America* (Reading, MA: Addison-Wesley, 1995), 230.

23. See Mark Levinson, "Wishful Thinking," and David Moberg, "Unions and the State," in *Boston Review*, February/March 2001: 13, 15.

terms by which environmental degradation is abated or remedied, as well as collaborate in local deliberative processes about managed growth and environmental sustainability. But such efforts, by themselves, can do little to affect broader environmental policies regarding acid rain, or global warming, or even the cessation of simple environmental point pollution. For this, there can be no substitute for a national (and indeed international) regulatory policy capable of articulating uniform standards and supporting well-funded and predictable regulatory enforcement. Yet such a policy requires a mobilization of resources and political will that simply does not currently exist. In such a setting, ongoing practices of production and consumption have a life of their own, generating a "mobilization of bias" in favor of environmental waste and degradation. The experience of the Chesapeake Bay Foundation is instructive here. The foundation is presented by Sirianni and Friedland as a model of civic environmentalism. It has joined together many local environmental and civic groups, across state boundaries, to call attention to environmental degradation and to promote collaborative stewardship of the Chesapeake Bay. And yet, as the *New York Times* recently reported, this exemplary effort to restore the Chesapeake Bay watershed continues to confront extraordinary obstacles. In 1987, the group committed itself to reducing nitrogen pollution by 40 percent. However, it has succeeded thus far in reducing it by only 17 percent because the group must contend not simply with the legacy of decades of uncontrolled pollution but also with an additional 300 *million* pounds of nitrogen pollution every year.[24]

The same limits present themselves, in an even more striking way, with regard to the problems of urban poverty and inequality. Even the most elaborate and well-connected civil society efforts come up against broad social trends, such as deindustrialization and suburban-

24. "Progress in Cleaning Chesapeake Bay, But Far to Go," *New York Times*, July 23, 2001: A12.

ization; massive social problems; and shortages of funds, bureaucratic delays, and the resistance of bankers, bondholders, corporate elites, and sometimes even municipal unions and social service agencies.[25] To offer just one example, the story of Sandtown, an inner-city neighborhood of Baltimore, is often cited as a civic renewal success story. An impressive partnership of city government, community organizations, and philanthropists supported a number of innovative housing, job training, youth development, and educational initiatives. And yet, as Peter Edelman—who has extolled this effort as a model—pointed out, these successes are limited and have come hard:

> Sandtown is still a poor neighborhood. Many of its adult residents are at a point where positive change is hard for them. There are still too many influences, both at home and on the street, that pull children in the wrong direction. Drug use seems to have actually increased. Nonmarital births are still four times the national rate. Two of the elementary schools have improved phenomenally, but it is not yet even near the truth to say that the school system is consistently turning out job-ready graduates from Sandtown. . . . The job situation is little better.[26]

Keep in mind that this is a civic renewal *success* story. Edelman's comments make clear how difficult success really is, even in those rare settings where "success" can plausibly be claimed at all.

In each of these domains, it would seem, we are presented with broad and systemic public problems whose solution would require equally broad and systemic public policy. Yet, what civil society offers tends to be ad hoc, localized, voluntarist, and often voluntary. What civil society offers is short on money and short on what political scientists call the "authoritative allocation of values." Authoritative

25. On these themes, see Matthew Filner, "On the Limits of Community Development: Participation, Power, and Growth in Urban America, 1965–Present," Ph.D. Dissertation, Department of Political Science, Indiana University, August 2001.

26. Peter Edelman, *Searching for America's Heart: RFK and the Renewal of Hope* (Boston: Houghton Mifflin, 2001), 197.

allocation is precisely what progressivism offered at the turn of the last century and what progressive public policy, in its subsequent iterations during the New Deal and Great Society periods, has always offered: a clear, coherent, national policy agenda for attacking social problems; for bringing them, as it were, to heel; and for substituting an overarching public purposiveness and public power for the anarchy of the market and the automatism of society.

To be sure, civil society efforts are genuine *efforts*. They mobilize a certain kind of civic power that is constituted by the concerted energies of diverse citizens working together. They tap practical idealism, they generate civic confidence, and they promote problem-solving experiences that are distinctive and worthy.[27] Such efforts do make a difference, but they do not typically mobilize *political power*. They do not generate organizational forms or ideological commitments that might render them capable of offsetting the power of privileged elites and of supporting a substantial political or policy agenda. To the extent that this is true, civil society efforts do not, and cannot, represent a solution to the problems that neoprogressives seek to address.[28]

Of course, few proponents of civil society would contend that voluntary efforts by themselves could succeed in solving pressing social problems. Even such conservative civil society advocates as Robert Woodson of the National Center for Neighborhood Enterprise recognize that governmental support for civil society efforts is indispensable to their success.[29] In every domain in which civil society

---

27. For a discussion of this kind of power, see Hannah Arendt, "On Violence," in *Crises of the Republic* (New York: Harcourt, 1972), especially 143–55.

28. Theda Skocpol makes this point in "Advocates Without Members," 499–506. See also Christopher Beem, *The Necessity of Politics: Reclaiming American Public Life* (Chicago: University of Chicago, 1999).

29. Robert L. Woodson Jr., "A Challenge to Conservatives," *Commonsense* 1, no. 3 (Summer 1994): 23–25. As Christopher Beem wrote: "The institutions of civil society are inherently ill suited to address some of the movement's core objectives. . . . [O]ur polity is best able to achieve the goals of the civil society movement when both the state and civil society are operative and vibrant, " in *The Necessity of*

initiatives have been lauded, it is fairly clear that these initiatives have thrived not as alternatives to public policy but as the beneficiaries of a supportive public policy. What Sirianni and Friedland observed about civic environmentalism is true in general: "it serves as a complement to, not a substitute for, regulation. A strong federal role is often required to trigger civic approaches."[30] But civil society advocates often fail to take the full measure of the significance of this reliance on public policy at a time of liberal political weakness. Sirianni and Friedland's *Civic Innovation in America* offers a case study of this failure, a failure that is all the more instructive because their book is the most empirically sound, careful, and discriminating account of such efforts to have emerged in the past decade.

Sirianni and Friedland catalogued a range of efforts that have emerged in four domains—community development, environmentalism, health policy, and public journalism. They insisted that these innovations are linked together in what they call a "broader civic renewal movement . . . with common language, shared practices, and networked relationships across a variety of arenas."[31] That these innovations share common themes—the importance of active citizenship, the danger of bureaucratism, the importance of pragmatic collaboration—seems clear, just as it seems clear that they are commonly promoted by a core network of philanthropies. The broader significance of these efforts, however, is less clear. Sirianni and Friedland seemed genuinely ambivalent here. On the one hand, their text is infused with an explicit "hopefulness" and with a sense that these civic innovations are transforming American public life. "Over the past decades," they wrote, "[Americans] have created forms of civic practice that are far more sophisticated in grappling with complex public problems and collaborating with highly diversified social actors than have ever existed in American history." Amid the worrisome signs of civic

---

Politics: Reclaiming American Public Life (Chicago: University of Chicago Press, 1999), 3.

30. Sirianni and Friedland, *Civic Innovation*, 85.

31. Ibid., 8.

disaffection documented by Robert Putnam and others, Sirianni and Friedland maintained, "there is already clear evidence of the kinds of civic innovation that could anchor and instruct broad revitalization strategies in the coming years."[32] The broad democratic promise of these efforts is the major theme of their text. On the other hand, they noted the serious difficulties confronting such a revitalization.

> We are deeply aware of the many obstacles that exist and the great uncertainty—even profound disagreement—about what a vital civic democracy might mean at the beginning of the twenty-first century. The story we tell is thus not only one of innovation and learning, but also one of roadblocks and detours, struggles and failures. Some of the failures, to be sure, have provided occasion for further learning, but others demonstrate the difficulty of bringing innovations to scale, embedding them in policy design, and creating a politics that will sustain them.[33]

When writing in this vein, they presented the broader project of democratic revitalization as a profoundly difficult task. They observed that "without a powerful movement capable of shifting the tides, too much of the vital public work and innovation of citizens analyzed in our core chapters will remain invisible and segmented, unable to inspire broad and vigorous commitment, and unable to redefine the underlying dynamics of 'politics as usual.'"[34] Here, the "movement for civic renewal" becomes something of a moral *imperative* rather than an existing state of affairs; and their argument, a call to arms rather than a descriptive account. It may be that without such a movement meaningful change will be impossible;[35] but this does not mean that such

32. Ibid., 1, 19.
33. Ibid., 9. See also p. 260, where they reiterate their view that the civic renewal "movement" has "achieved an important threshold of recognition in the media," but then note that "nonetheless, these important foundational accomplishments over a decade should not be exaggerated, nor the obstacles to further development of a broad movement underestimated."
34. Ibid., 33–34.
35. Ibid., 27–71.

a movement is likely to be forthcoming. Like Harry Boyte's earlier *Backyard Revolution*, which, as they acknowledged, first made the case more than two decades ago for the importance of such civil society efforts, *Civic Innovation in America* is not simply an analysis but rather a brief for a particular vision of civic renewal, whereby a broad convergence of interest is anticipated and endorsed.[36] This hopefulness cannot simply be dismissed. The innovations in question *could* anchor "broad revitalization strategies," but these innovations might *not* have this effect. That these efforts together even make up a "movement" is far from clear.

A political movement typically involves more than certain common symbolic frames and some degree of overlapping memberships. It also involves a common substantive vision and a sense of historical destiny and forward *movement* toward the achievement of this vision. A political movement, arguably, requires a *teleology*, a grand narrative within which particular efforts acquire larger meaning[37]—early twentieth-century progressivism had this; so did New Deal liberalism. It is not clear that the civic efforts Siranni and Friedland discuss share any such teleology. They admitted as much, explicitly underscoring what sets the civic renewal movement apart from other social movements of the past and what constitutes its genuine distinctiveness:

> Because the civic renewal movement is not primarily a rights or justice movement, it cannot rely on the metaphors, frames, strategies, or tactical repertoires of recent democratic movements. It cannot inspire action on the basis of unconditional claims to rights or righteous struggles against clearly defined oppressors. . . . It cannot capture and focus public attention through mass protests, marches on Washington, boycotts, strikes, freedom rides, and sit-ins, nor can it count on repression by authorities to galvanize widespread

36. See Harry Boyte, *The Backyard Revolution: Understanding the New Citizen Movement* (Philadelphia: Temple University Press, 1980).

37. My argument here is indebted to Richard Rorty's essay "Movements and Campaigns." *Dissent*, Winter 1995: 55–60.

support. It cannot expect dramatic court decisions to energize activists or to secure significant new levers of power and representation. . . . And while legislation could certainly enact "policy designs for democracy" that help build civic capacity in specific areas, a civic renewal movement cutting across many institutional sectors cannot hope to build its networks through advocacy coalitions and lobbying for specific laws.[38]

This analysis suggests that while civil society efforts surely make up *something* worth emulating, they do not necessarily make a movement at all but rather a heterogeneous, pluralistic, fractious assemblage of particular and local activities and aspirations, with little political unity or historical directionality whatsoever. This sense is further reinforced by Sirianni and Friedland's insistence that the "movement" is, and ought to remain, beyond partisan political competition. While they clearly leaned toward the Democratic Party, believing it the most suitable partisan vehicle of civic initiative, they insisted that what is most distinctive about civic renewal is its communitarian, collaborative, and pragmatic ethos. Such civil society efforts, they insisted, draw their energy from a sense of civic responsibility that is, in important respects, *antipolitical.* Direct linkage to conventional political organizations and movements "has little relevance to the work of civic renewal that needs to occur in all kinds of institutional and professional settings, from schools, universities, and hospitals to corporations, social service nonprofits, and public agencies. Meeting the major challenges in these settings . . . has little to gain from politicization and much to lose." For, according to Sirianni and Friedland, direct politicization encourages adversarial, rather than collaborative, orientations; it encourages "rights talk" and other insistent discourses about justice and injustice and the political remediation of wrong; and it focuses too much of its energy on the satisfaction of "interests that can be served by state regulatory, social welfare, and redistributive policies."[39] Politicization, in other words, implicates a progressive lib-

38. Sirianni and Friedland, *Civic Innovation*, 272–73.
39. Ibid., 264–65.

eral project that Sirianni and Friedland considered outmoded and indeed counterproductive, not only because it requires the empowerment of bureaucratic state institutions but also because it is likely to generate powerful political opposition.

In making this argument Sirianni and Friedland's book merges into the broader discourse of the third way, which has risen to prominence in the past decade largely in connection with the electoral victories, and policy agendas, of Bill Clinton and Tony Blair. The "third way" is a slogan that has been deployed, with substantial effect, by American New Democrat and British New Labour politicians seeking political power in societies that had experienced the electoral defeat of progressive or social democratic parties and the political ascendancy of Reaganite and Thatcherite conservatism. Sidney Blumenthal, erstwhile Clintonite, described the third way as "the practical experience of two leading politicians [Clinton and Blair] who win elections, operate in the real world, and understand the need, in a global economy, to find common solutions for common problems." Beneath the slogan, the third way connotes both a political strategy and a policy agenda. The political strategy is to move, in the words of Anthony Giddens, "beyond left and right," and to seek a broad consensus in the center of the political spectrum, at what is called, interchangeably, the "radical center," the "vital center," and the "active middle."[40] The basic point of this strategy is to acknowledge that neither progressive liberalism nor social democratic reformism can any longer rely on the support of an organized and powerful working class. Both must instead make their accommodation with the forces of deindustrialization and suburbanization and the hegemony

40. See Anthony Giddens, *Beyond Left and Right: The Future of Radical Politics* (Stanford, CA: Stanford University Press, 1994); and Giddens, *The Third Way* (London: Polity Press, 1998). See also Jeffrey Isaac, "The Road (Not?) Taken: Anthony Giddens, The Third Way, and the Future of Social Democracy," *Dissent*, Spring 2001: 61–70.

of market values that have weakened working-class solidarities.[41] Accompanying this strategy is a policy agenda associated with the retrenchment of the welfare state and the politics of national regulation and an effort to actively promote the opportunities associated with private markets, third-wave technologies, and third-sector philanthropic activity. In the name of flexibility, third-wave politics endorses a dramatic scaling back of the role of the national state and a virtual repudiation of the progressive legacy in the name of progress itself.

In the United States, this third way has been associated with the Democratic Leadership Council and the Progressive Policy Institute under the leadership of Al Fromm and Will Marshall, respectively. Marshall nicely summarized this third-wave approach in an essay, "A New Fighting Faith," published in the DLC's *New Democrat* in support of the Clinton reelection campaign:

> The party's old faith, New Deal progressivism, has run its historic course. In his January State of the Union address, President Clinton made it official when he declared that "the era of big government is over." The venerable New Deal creed was undone both by its great success in creating a large middle class that now sees itself more burdened than benefited from government, and by its undue reliance on outdated bureaucracies and top-down programs to meet the needs of a fast changing society. . . . For today's progressives, there is no challenge more compelling than the need to replace a governance model developed for the Industrial Age—an era characterized by large, centralized institutions. . . . The new paradigm for progressive government springs from a simple insight: since we can no longer rely on big institutions to take care of us, we must create policies and institutions that enable us to take care of ourselves."[42]

41. See William A. Galston and Elaine C. Kamarck, "Five Realities That Will Shape 21st Century US Politics," reprinted in Anthony Giddens, ed., *The Global Third Way Debate* (Cambridge, Eng.: Polity Press, 2001).

42. Will Marshall, "A New Fighting Faith," *New Democrat* 8, no. 5 (September/ October 1996): 14–15.

Marshall's so-called new progressivism thus repudiates a strong state and a vigorous public policy in the name of equal opportunity, mutual responsibility, and self-governing citizenship. In the place of a supposedly heavy-handed and sclerotic state, the New Democrats exalt voluntarism, in economics, ethics, trade policy, social regulation, and social service delivery. For Marshall, this new progressivism is a partisan strategy suited to Democratic electoral victories.[43] But the affinities between this approach and the "new citizenship" endorsed by such "compassionate conservatives" as Michael Joyce, Michael Woodson, and William Schambra, who are closely associated with the political agenda of the Republican Party under the leadership of George W. Bush, should be obvious. These compassionate conservatives tend to be *civic* Republicans who sound the same themes— fiscal austerity, social solidarity, and civic engagement—as their New Democratic counterparts.[44] The new citizenship is, ideologically speaking, a *bipartisan* approach well adapted to a political terrain characterized by liberal exhaustion and substantial conservative success in delegitimizing a progressive agenda.[45]

Instructive in this regard is the Reinventing Citizenship Project organized in 1993 by William Galston, a prominent political theorist, long-time Democratic issues adviser, and White House Deputy Assistant for Domestic Policy in Clinton's first term. Under Galston's leadership, this project brought together many of the academic and civic leaders of the civic renewal movement. It organized meetings,

43. See Kenneth S. Baer, *Reinventing Democrats: The Politics of Liberalism from Clinton to Reagan* (Lawrence: Kansas University Press, 2000).

44. See, for example, Don E. Eberly, ed., *Building a Community of Citizens: Civil Society in the 21st Century* (Lanham, MD: University Press of America, 1994); and Stephen Goldsmith, *The Twenty-First Century City: Resurrecting Urban America* (Lanham, MD: Rowman & Littlefield, 2002).

45. This convergence was noted in Herbert Wray, et al., "The revival of civic life." *US News & World Reports*, January 29, 1996. See also Craig R. Rimmerman, *The New Citizenship: Unconventional Politics, Activism, and Service* (Boulder, CO: Westview Press, 1997).

conducted public hearings, published reports, and drafted policy proposals and public declarations on the themes of civic renewal and reinventing citizenship. Sirianni and Friedland—active participants in this process—described the effort with a measure of legitimate enthusiasm, which seems legitimate because the project involved many interesting people and ideas and seemed to signify a real openness to civic innovation at the highest levels of government. But they offer only a single sentence by way of an account of the ultimate political fate of these noble efforts: "The administration, however, proved unable to focus on this and other related initiatives once the congressional elections of 1994 took center stage."[46] They do note that the White House continued to consult with academics linked to the civic renewal discourse and that it even "fashioned active citizenship themes" for use in the 1995 State of the Union and the 1996 presidential campaign. However, there does not appear to have been any White House follow-through or policy outcome associated with the project. For the Clinton administration, "reinventing citizenship" appears to have been a theme rather than a political vision.[47] As a rhetoric, new citizenship themes have clearly served a Democratic Party leadership intent on unburdening liberalism of its progressive liberal past, dismantling the welfare state, promoting global free trade, and emphasizing the assumption of civic duties at a time when there seems to be little political interest in enforcing social or economic rights.

At the same time, it is important to note that if the new citizenship was for the Clinton administration primarily a theme, its distinctive features *as* a rhetoric at least deserve note. In a political

46. Sirianni and Friedland, *Civic Innovation*, 250. My account of the Reinventing Citizenship Project draws largely from Sirianni and Friedland's account but also from the texts posted on the Civic Practices Network website.

47. This is also the chastened conclusion of Benjamin Barber, who, like Sirianni and Friedland, was an active participant in the Reinventing Citizenship Project. See Barber's recent book *The Truth of Power: Intellectual Affairs in the Clinton White House* (New York: Norton, 2001).

context in which social Darwinist themes have played an important role in delegitimizing liberalism, and in which forms of ethnic and religious fundamentalism have come to prevail throughout many parts of the world, the discourse of new citizenship and civic responsibility emphatically articulates liberal and universalist values. The appeal to civility is no grand answer to the problems confronting American society, but it is to be preferred to rhetorics of incivility that demonize or villify particular groups and essentialize individual competition and social conflict. At the same time, however, when this appeal is not accompanied by a serious and coherent policy agenda at a time of intensified social and economic insecurity, it can easily assume a moralizing tone that smacks of hypocrisy—something from which new citizenship discourse has too often suffered.[48]

This is not to say that the third way is a politics of betrayal. To the contrary, the third way represents a savvy political strategy of coming to terms with changed social and political conditions. Those who charge New Democrats with betrayal, however sincere they may be, fail to reckon with these changes. As Lars-Erik Nelson pointed out, Bill Clinton—the only truly successful Democratic presidential politician since the mid-1960s—was never a left or progressive Democrat. He was a moderate governor of a Southern state who was elected to office in 1992 with 43 percent of the popular vote—hardly a mandate for progressive change. He had already demonstrated his commitment to the DLC strategy of modernizing the Democratic Party by shifting it to the Right. He was supported by the smallest congressional majority of any president elected in the twentieth century. And he confronted a Republican Party that had moved far to the Right and that had successfully shifted political discourse to the

48. This is the theme of Benjamin DeMott's provocative *The Trouble With Friendship: Why Americans Can't Think Straight About Race* (New Haven, CT: Yale University Press, 2000).

Right. In Nelson's words, "[T]here was a great political middle to be grabbed, and Clinton grabbed it."[49]

Clinton may well have betrayed his own idealistic rhetorical flourishes, and he surely treated the rhetorics of liberalism and civic responsibility in an opportunistic fashion that demoralized many who took seriously his rhetoric of renewal. Further, he surely made tactical mistakes—most notably regarding health care reform—that may have limited his subsequent ability to live up to even a small portion of the promise that many originally attached to his presidency. But, given the balance of political forces that were arrayed behind him and against him, it is hard to imagine him performing much differently than he did.[50] Like most politicians, he took the path of least resistance to electoral success. If that path was essentially a neoliberal one, this can hardly be blamed on Clinton because there existed little backing for anything more progressive and many obstacles were in the way of a more ambitious agenda. Clinton is not without blame for many of his failings, but neither is Clinton the demiurgic betrayer of liberalism that many of his critics on the left believe him to be. He was, simply, a creature of his times—a Democratic leader at a time when the sources of liberal vigor had dried up and the Democratic Party had become, for all intents and purposes, Republican. Clinton surely aided and abetted this transsubstantiation, but he was hardly its prime mover.[51]

Similarly, to note the affinities between the discourse of civic

49. Lars-Erik Nelson, "Clinton and His Enemies," *New York Review of Books*, January 20, 2000: 20.

50. This argument is brilliantly made by Theda Skocpol in her *Boomerang: Clinton's Health Security Effort and the Turn Against Government in U.S. Politics* (New York: W. W. Norton, 1996).

51. On this matter, see the fascinating exchange between Robert Kuttner and E. J. Dionne Jr., "Did Clinton Succeed or Fail?" *American Prospect*, August 28, 2000: 42–46. See also Stephen Skowronek's discussion of Clinton's "preemptive" third way politics, in *The Politics Presidents Make: Leadership From John Adams to Bill Clinton* (Cambridge, MA: Harvard University Press, 1997), 447–64.

renewal and the third way policies of the New Democratic Clinton administration is to impugn neither the motives nor the achievements of the proponents of civic renewal. I agree with Sirianni and Friedland, and indeed with Will Marshall and other proponents of third way thinking, that progressive liberalism is largely anachronistic, the product of economic and political conditions that no longer pertain. I also agree that meaningful partisan political contention in American national politics is likely to take place in the "active middle," on the terrain of a consensus on the impracticality of ambitious social democratic regulation, the virtues of economic globalization and the market, and the centrality of a civic politics centered on social solidarity and voluntarism rather than on vigorous politicized demands for socioeconomic justice.[52]

In such an environment, collaborative approaches often have the greatest chance of practical success, and partisan entanglement often promises little reward for civil society initiatives—political vision or substantial funding seem forthcoming from neither party—and many costs. At the same time, once one presumes that the policy debate is severely constricted, it seems advisable to work, pragmatically, with all those—conservative and liberal, religious and secular, business-oriented and labor-oriented—who are committed to practical solutions to public problems. In the domains of neighborhood and community organizing, civic environmentalism, the experimental practice of deliberative democracy in local settings, philanthropic activity (especially United Way fund-raising, which is a major source of social service funding in most American local communities), and even faith-based initiatives in social service delivery, there exist collaborative opportunities to work effectively across partisan and ideological boundaries.[53] Such work may not be where the partisan political action is, and it

52. This is also the argument of Ted Halsted and Michael Lind's *The Radical Center: The Future of American Politics* (New York: Doubleday, 2001).

53. See Jeffrey Isaac, "Faith-Based Initiatives: A Civil Society Approach," *The Good Society*, Summer 2002.

is a far cry from more ambitious visions of policy innovation and political transformation, but it is most assuredly where much of the civic energy and action really *is* in American society today. It would be sheer foolishness to deny this.

My problem is not with the civil society focus of the partisans of civic renewal, nor with the disposition of these partisans to discern promise in such collaborative efforts. Rather, it is with the celebratory and credulous tone with which much of this tends to be discussed by civic renewal writers. For although these writers display great knowledge about the rhetorics and tactics of civic renewal, they tend to be too buoyant in their view of what such efforts can and do accomplish. Committed to the agency of ordinary citizens and to the importance of civic self-understandings and purposes, these writers assume the role of civic storytellers, whose task it is to relate inspiring tales of civic innovation that might extend and deepen future innovation. This is an admirable task. The closer one gets to the ground of activism, the more one may feel called to this task of civic self-promotion. Such a vocation, however, substitutes an interest in meaning for an interest in *causality and consequence*. What is lacking in much of the civic renewal literature is a serious reckoning with the causal *constraints* under which civil society efforts operate. These constraints, which severely limit the chances of reviving a progressive policy agenda, also limit the aspirations of civic renewal.

The Sisyphean Task of Civil Society Politics

Thus, civil society efforts both do and do not offer an alternative to more progressive aspirations. They are promising examples of civic initiative and pragmatic problem solving. They may well be the only game in town. But they are limited, and frustrating, in ways that civic renewal advocates rarely admit. The problem with the discourse of civil society is not its post-progressivism but its *credulity*, its failure to see the *tragedy* in the decline of progressive liberalism. Civic renewal writers of the Left and the Right—and for the partisans of civic renewal, these lines are increasingly blurred—properly discern the poverty of progressivism and properly seek to discern the redeeming promise in progressivism's decline. They rightly appreciate the innovative character of contemporary civil society efforts, which are the products of genuine learning experiences among activists and elites in the post-1960s period. But they present as an unambiguous gain what is in fact a problematic achievement. They insufficiently consider the fact that these efforts are largely the product of learning *under severe duress* and that this duress is due to the political weakening of progressive forces. This duress has created not only new opportunities and flexibilities but also new *vulnerabilities* and anxieties.

While the welfare state surely had its pathologies, the decline of the progressive agenda has unleashed the equally potent pathologies of the private sphere, including the pathologies of civil society itself: Privatism. Insularity. Greed. Self-absorption. Exclusivism. Ethnic, racial, and sexual resentment. These pathologies cannot simplistically be laid at the feet of a bureaucratic state or the social engineering aspirations of progressive elites. They are features of contemporary civil society, which is not a pristine or communitarian site of smooth and edifying social interaction and need satisfaction.[54] The "liberation" of society from social regulation represents not only a defeat of bureaucracy but also a serious eclipse of public agencies and identities. The new citizenship this has called forth embodies genuine civic impulses, but its very voluntarism and its partiality serve to vitiate one of the most important features of modern liberal democratic citizenship—its universality. Civil society's gain has thus been civil society's loss—a loss of material resources and of the ethical and civic resources associated with a serious commitment to universal citizenship and social justice on the part of the state acting in the name of

---

54. On this theme, see Simone Chambers and Jeffrey Kopstein, "Bad Civil Society," *Political Theory* 29, no. 6 (December 2001): 837–66.

society as a whole. Civil society discourse typically lacks any appreciation of the *tragedy* of this.

Similarly, although civic renewal may not be strictly a partisan affair, the current partisan *stasis* is hardly supportive of independent civic initiative. While third way liberals and their compassionate conservative compatriots offer rhetorical support for social responsibility and civic engagement, they do not offer a coherent program for supporting civil society initiative on a level commensurate with the problems confronting society today. Yet, at the same time, their neoliberal economic commitments help generate many of the problems against which ordinary citizens and grassroots civic associations set themselves. In this context, moral invocations of civility, voluntarism, and the importance of a sacrificial ethos ring hollow.[55] Civil society needs more than moral earnestness; it needs a great deal of *help*. The most honest partisans of civic renewal acknowledge this, as do many neo-progressives, such as Theda Skocpol, E. J. Dionne Jr., and Margaret Weir, who have sought to critically engage the partisans of civil society in dialogue about the necessary reliance of civic renewal upon public policy.[56]

What this means is that *the political crisis of progressive liberalism is a problem of enormous proportions for civic renewal*. It is not something that can be ignored on the grounds that civic politics is nonpartisan or beyond Left and Right. The situation may well be beyond Left, but *it is not beyond Right*. Conservative economic policies have dominated, and continue to dominate, party-political discourse. American politics today operates on the terrain of triumphant market values and institutions.[57] However, this is not a natural or ineluctable

55. See, for example, Stephen Carter, *Civility* (New York: Harper, 1977).
56. See, for example, Margaret Weir and Marshall Ganz, "Reconnecting People and Politics," in Stanley B. Greenberg and Theda Skocpol, eds., *The New Majority: Toward a Popular Progressive Politics* (New Haven, CT: Yale University Press, 1997).
57. For a perceptive, if exaggerated, argument to this effect, see Thomas Frank, *One Market Under God: Extreme Capitalism, Market Populism, and the End of Economic Democracy* (New York: Doubleday, 2000).

development or a simple actualization of freedom; it is a *problematic historical outcome.* Civil society is a solution that is not commensurate with this problem; yet it may be the only viable solution in the sense that no other method of practical response is viable.

There is no point in denying this tragic bind or seeking an easy way out of it. An honest reading of the political situation suggests that the prospects for a progressive revival are dim. This does not mean, however, that efforts to craft political coalitions and movements designed to move beyond the current situation and generate a new progressive hegemony are hopeless. If it would be foolish to credulously anticipate a new progressive dispensation, it would be no less foolish to adopt a posture of dogmatic incredulity. The truth is that we cannot confidently predict the future. Things may change. Progressive forces may strengthen. A crisis might precipitate the turn toward a more radical agenda—though this may just as likely be a radicalism of the Right as of the Left. The most appropriate approach to such scenarios is simply an experimental openness to new possibilities. However, this experimental openness should consist of more than willful optimism. It should draw on a sober historical and social analysis combined with a chastened sense of political realism.

Such a sense of realism would caution against optimism, but it would not counsel political despair. Although the national political landscape is bleak, there currently exist some promising examples of seemingly successful efforts to create new progressively oriented coalitions at the state and local level. In Milwaukee, for example, the Campaign for a Sustainable Milwaukee, a coalition of more than 100 labor and citizen groups, has worked to achieve substantial influence over the city council and to promote regional planning, job training, and living wage initiatives. In Burlington, Vermont, a progressive coalition of socialists and liberal Democrats has been able to advance an impressive policy agenda centered around left-liberal values. In Connecticut, the Legislative Electoral Action Program has successfully run citizen-activist candidates for the state legislature, in the process building a base for political and economic reform. In New York, the Working Families Party, a fusion party formed by progressive unions and such activist citizens' organizations as ACORN and Citizen Action, has achieved some modest headway through its cross-endorsements of liberal Democratic candidates. In cities across the United States, from Boston to Portland (Oregon) to Baltimore, living wage campaigns linking unions, citizens, and liberal politicians have successfully instituted "living wage ordinances," raising the wage rates of city-contracted workers and enhancing the local influence of unions.[58]

Each of these efforts involves the mobilization of party organizations and the winning of electoral offices; and each contains promise. But to date, these efforts have had a limited effect on national politics, at the level of political discourse, party agendas, or public policy. Each also confronts political obstacles, particularly once they are extended beyond local contexts and treated as models of national renewal. The original progressivism emerged out of disparate local tumult and experimentation; historical conditions at the turn of the twentieth century supported this emergence. In retrospect, we can understand how and why such a progressive coalescence occurred. Unfortunately, historical conditions today do not appear similarly supportive.

America in Search of a Public Philosophy?

What then of politics understood as the practice of public decision making oriented toward a conception of the public good? Is the very idea of "public good" anachronistic? Is it necessary for the diverse efforts noted above to add up to something larger, more visionary, or

58. See Jay Walljasper, "Burlington, Northern Light," *Nation*, May 19, 1997: 18–23; Bruce Shapiro, "Rappaport Makes the LEAP," *Nation*, September 21, 1998: 27–28; Micah Sifry, "A Working Third Party," *Nation*, November 6, 2000; Harold Meyerson, "California's Progressive Mosaic." *American Prospect* 12, no. 11 (June 18, 2001); and Michael H. Shuman, "Going Local: Devolution for Progressives," *Nation*, October 12, 1998.

more edifying? Do we need what the political philosopher Michael Sandel called a new "public philosophy" of citizenship, capable of inspiring citizens to undertake collective projects and of orienting them toward greater, more substantial, inclusive commonalities?

Sandel was notably ambivalent on this score. On the one hand, he supported a "political agenda informed by civic concerns" and of a "formative project" of engaged, republican citizenship that is intimated, "hinted," and "gestured" at by current civic renewal initiatives.[59] The entire thrust of his book *Democracy's Discontent* is to criticize the inadequacies of contemporary post-1960s liberalism as a materialistic and individualistic "public philosophy" and to suggest the desirability of an alternative, "republican" philosophy of public life. On the other hand, he was quite vague about both the substance of such a philosophy and the collective agents or institutional forms capable of bringing it into existence. Although he briefly mentioned many of the initiatives discussed above, he admitted that they are "disparate expressions" of citizenship and that they exist "around the edges of our political discourse and practice."

A similar ambivalence haunts Robert Putnam's *Bowling Alone*. Having analyzed at great length the current "disappearance of civic America," Putnam concluded by considering "What Is to Be Done?" He maintained that "we desperately need an era of civic inventiveness to create a renewed set of institutions and channels for a reinvigorated civic life that will fit the way we have come to live. Our challenge now is to reinvent the twenty-first century equivalent of the Boy Scouts or the settlement house of the United Mine Workers or the NAACP." We need such innovation, Putnam insisted, both to restore civic confidence and because social capital is "not an alternative to, but a prerequisite for, political mobilization and reform."[60] Putnam issued a sermonic call for civic invention and "social capitalism" in

59. Michael Sandel, *Democracy's Discontent: America in Search of a Public Philosophy* (Cambridge, MA: Harvard University Press, 1996), 324, 333, 338.
60. Putnam, *Bowling Alone*, 401, 399.

six domains. He desired that the renewal of "social capital" should become a unifying political project. He sought a convergence of interest in renewal on the part of all of those active in civic life. Yet, he offered no political account of how or why this convergence might occur.

There are good reasons to believe that such a convergence is not likely to occur. Beyond this, however, there is something peculiar about the very desire to promote such a convergence. What is most distinctive about civil society as a site of civic engagement is precisely its associational plurality, which resists clear political representation. Labor, religious, environmental, community, racial, and other associations form in civil society and operate there on a voluntary and particularistic basis, without any necessary or clear overarching political goals. Sometimes such groups form coalitions or work in tandem. Sometimes they work at cross purposes with each other. Civically active women might join together in support of a local soup kitchen or county museum or the Girl Scouts; and yet some may support Planned Parenthood or the National Abortion Rights Action League, while others support "family values" groups or anti-abortion crisis pregnancy centers. Religious congregations and clergy groups might join together to celebrate Martin Luther King Jr. Day and yet disagree strongly on the topic of gay rights. A range of community groups— neighborhood associations, environmental organizations, labor unions, League of Women Voters, chambers of commerce, various trade and civic associations—may come together to support organizing forums of "public deliberation" about the economic future of their community, and yet they may sharply diverge when it comes to the initiatives and policies they are willing to support. If the site of political innovation today is in the domain of civil society, and if this domain is inherently complex and multivocal, then perhaps it is pointless to hope for some Hegelian synthesis to emerge from it.

Along these lines, the record of the Industrial Areas Foundation (IAF) is instructive. The IAF is a fascinating example of a successful civic initiative that is informed by a robust conception of democratic participation. Its combination of idealism and effectiveness explains why many contemporary writers regarded it as exemplary.[61] In his recent book, Mark R. Warren presented the most careful account of the IAF written thus far.[62] Focusing on the successes of IAF organizer Ernesto Cortes Jr., Warren charted the development of an elaborate community-organizing network, rooted in the power of San Antonio's Communities Organized for Public Service (COPS), which has extended throughout the state of Texas and indeed has developed a broader presence in the Southwest region as a whole. IAF organizations are broad based, rooted in local institutions and faith communities, and created on the basis of painstaking face-to-face contact, discussion, and public work. They engage in voluntary community-building initiatives. But they also practice grassroots political organizing, deploying tactics of nonpartisan political pressure and carefully planned protest to focus public attention on the plight of disadvantaged communities and to demand, and achieve, governmental responses in areas ranging from garbage collection and sewage disposal to affordable housing to public school reform, job training, and employment.

Warren demonstrated that IAF organizing has been effective because it is centered in local institutions and dedicated to grassroots capacity building. He concluded:

> It is quite easy to dismiss this local organizing in the face of the globalization of the economy. Many analysts jump immediately to

61. See for example William Grieder, *Who Will Tell The People* (New York: Touchstone, 1992), 222–44; Harry Boyte and Nancy Kari, *Building America: The Democratic Promise of Public Work* (Philadelphia: Temple University Press, 1996), 145–46; Sandel, *Democracy's Discontent*, 336–38; Sirianni and Friedland, *Civic Innovation in America*, 35–84; William Julius Wilson, *The Bridge Over the Racial Divide* (Berkeley: University of California Press, 1999), 85–92; and Putnam, *Bowling Alone*, 68.

62. Mark R. Warren, *Dry Bones Rattling: Community Building to Revitalize American Democracy* (Princeton, NJ: Princeton University Press, 2001).

an effort to figure out the correct policy, the right issue, to solve local problems. Activists rush to influence the highest levels of power. To do so is a serious mistake. Political and policy elites have much to offer our understanding of public policy, but they can't operate alone. Grand schemes launched by Washington-based advocacy groups often lack the organized backing to be adopted in the political arena. They are not necessarily the most effective policies anyway. Local knowledge, a close understanding of the needs and aspirations of Americans at the ground level, must inform social policy if it is to be effective.[63]

Nonetheless, Warren also recognized the limits of such organizing, contending that "high-level power is still required" to facilitate such local efforts and to develop public policies commensurate with the problems confronting ordinary American citizens. He also noted that "the relentless emphasis on local work . . . has left the IAF ill equipped to undertake national action now that it has the foundation to do so." Like Sandel and Putnam, Warren nourished a lingering hope that the successes of the IAF could be replicated on a national level and that the IAF might serve as a model for a "national force for political renewal."[64]

Warren correctly noted the limits of IAF strategies and observed that some kind of national renewal would be necessary to more vigorously and comprehensively address the problems of urban America. But his expectation that the IAF might somehow anticipate such a renewal seems to fly in the face of his own analysis of the IAF's distinctiveness. The IAF has sought to develop power locally and to exercise this power in ways that are experimental and issue-specific and that forswear the establishment of permanent alliances or the identification of permanent adversaries. Such an improvisational modus operandi does not lend itself to national forms of organization,

63. Ibid., 254.
64. Ibid., 256, 262.

to mass politics, or to ambitious programs of national renewal and redistributive social policy.

If the IAF is exemplary, it is precisely because of its unique and pragmatic combination of civic audacity and programmatic modesty. It should best be viewed not as a model of civic innovation to be replicated on a larger scale but rather as an example of effective civic innovation under arduous conditions. Models can be reiterated, replicated, and expanded; examples can only be emulated. To view the IAF as an example is to acknowledge that it is not an all-purpose guide to civic initiative nor the harbinger of something bigger and better. It simply exemplifies some important principles and pragmatic understandings that are worth amplifying and that might be the basis for a range of efforts across a range of domains. My point is not that the IAF should forswear efforts to organize and to expand its influence in new places, but that it would be a mistake to overburden the IAF with large-scale political expectations that exceed its capacities and that obscure its distinctive modalities and achievements.

What I am suggesting is that the IAF furnishes a useful example of what politics in America today can accomplish. As such, it can be a touchstone for a new political orientation, but less as an integrative public philosophy or agenda than as an ethos of pragmatic public engagement. Such an ethos would promote the value of individual and associational freedom and encourage the exercise of this freedom by conscientious citizens and civic groups. It would foster an appreciation for the pluralism that is endemic to modern social life while promoting civility and the inclination to engage, rather than demonize, one's adversaries. It would advance the values of civic equality and social solidarity, which entail that a political community is more than a war of each against all and that questions of inequality of opportunity or advantage are public questions that involve some measure of public responsibility. Most especially, it would promote the idea of democracy itself—the idea that ordinary citizens ought to take responsibility for the problems of their world and ought to collaborate in crafting, implementing, and monitoring public solutions to these problems. However, it would be distinguished not by the way it philosophically configures these values nor by an integrated vision of public policy believed to actualize these values. Instead, it would be distinguished by the understanding that as a matter of politics, there is no single "best" way to articulate and advance these values.

Instead of anticipating some new integrated vision of public life, we should attend to the range of experiments, initiatives, and organizations that currently exist and are likely to grow. These are not likely to be informed by a common vision, and they are not likely to converge upon a common vision. They are likely to function in a hostile political environment in which social and economic "progress" is the source not only of advantage but also of difficulty, disappointment, and risk and in which national political organizations and state institutions are incapable of generating either the public vision or the political will to bring such problems to heel.

To propose this is not to dismiss or disparage more hopeful scenarios and projects. Hopefulness, visionary thinking, and ambitious policy agendas have their place in politics. Without them, democratic politics could never rise above the prosaic and the banal. Without them, democratic politics could never have begun to institute social justice and progressive social policy. But hopefulness and vision also have the potential to limit political thinking by furnishing a measure of optimism and comfort where it is not warranted and by encouraging a kind of overreaching that can be dispiriting and self-defeating. The comfort of neoprogressivism is the belief that historical forces are tending in a progressive direction and that a sufficient grasp of these forces can unlock the strategic key to progressive triumph. The comfort of the partisans of civil society is that the prose of everyday civic life is sufficient to sustain public problem solving and civic renewal. But both forms of credulity are mistaken. History does not bode well for progressivism, but neither is a robust civil society sufficient to redeem what Herbert Croly called the promise of American life. The irony is that at this moment of American celebration, this promise may be, in crucial respects, beyond redemption.

The asymmetry between the problems we confront and the likely means of their solution should not be a cause for despair. Democratic energies and vehicles for the partial realization of these solutions continue to exist, and these warrant critical support. The values they embody ought to be elucidated, publicized, and made the topic of civic self-reflection and civic education. Citizens who engage in them can experience a sense of efficacy and perhaps some measure of practical satisfaction, but they are also bound to experience such efforts as limited, partial, and frustrating. Learning to live with these frustrations, and to persist without resentment in spite of them, may prove to be the most important civic virtue of our time.

In Albert Camus's novel *The Plague*, Dr. Rieux, the heroic leader of the resistance, is asked what gives him the confidence to persist in his struggle against an injustice that seems virtually implacable. "I've no more," he responds, "than the pride that's needed to keep me going. I have no idea what's awaiting me, or what will happen when all this ends. For the moment I know this: there are sick people and they need curing." The world, he avers, is bounded by death, and our victories on behalf of life are always temporary, always fragile. "Yet this is not reason," he concludes, "for giving up the struggle." Camus's Rieux is a slightly more heroic version of Sisyphus, who also confronts a tragic fate. Sisyphus is doomed to persist, without end, in the impossible task of raising his stone to the top of the mountain. His fate is to fail. Such a fate could well cause him to despair. But on Camus's telling, Sisyphus learns that it is not the mountaintop but the rock that is his true fate. His universe henceforth "seems to him neither sterile nor futile. Each atom of that stone, each mineral flake of that night-filled mountain, in itself forms a world. The struggle toward the heights is enough to fill a man's heart. One must imagine Sisyphus happy." Sisyphus's happiness is a tragic happiness, but it is more than despair because Sisyphus is motivated by a value—

the value of his own agency—and so motivated, his struggle, and its always inadequate results, has meaning. Those who interpret the myth of Sisyphus as a story of futility are mistaken, for it is only from the standpoint of the mountaintop that Sisyphus fails.

American democracy faces severe challenges. I do not think that we can, in good faith, confront the present century with the same optimism and ambition with which progressives confronted the last one. The kinds of democratic responses that are likely to be effective are bound to be partial, limiting, fractious, and in many ways unsatisfying. They are likely to disappoint the modernist quest for mastery and the progressive faith in the future. And they are likely to frustrate the democratic project of collective self-control and self-governance. Yet it is the great virtue of democracy as a form of politics that it prizes contingency, experimentation, critique, and further experimentation, ad infinitum. For, in the end, politics, even under the most favorable circumstances, is nothing else but the Sisyphean task of constructing provisional solutions to our unmasterable difficulties.

Varieties of Conservatism in America
Edited by Peter Berkowitz

Although conservatives may all look alike to their critics, they disagree among themselves about what it means to be a conservative and who is entitled to bear the name. This book examines the questions that divide conservatives today and presents the variety of answers put forward by classical conservatives, libertarians, and neoconservatives.

The contributors—drawn from varied professional backgrounds—each bring a distinctive voice to bear, illustrating the book's overarching argument that conservatism in America represents a family of opinions and ideas rather than a rigid doctrine or settled creed. At the same time, the contributors clarify the moral underpinnings of the varieties of American conservatism and shed light on the political implications of each variety.

The essays in this volume demonstrate that the debate among conservatives about which principles and practices are most urgently in need of protection is also a debate with and within that larger liberalism that undergirds the American constitutional order. The essays suggest as well that this larger liberalism, with its bedrock devotion to individual liberty and equality before the law, serves as the common ground on which the contending camps within conservatism—and indeed conservatives in their contentions with progressives—can come together, debate civilly, and discover ways to advance the public good.

Peter Berkowitz teaches at George Mason University School of Law and is a fellow at the Hoover Institution. He is the author of two books, and the editor of several books including the companion to this volume, *Varieties of Progressivism in America.*

Contributors: Randy E. Barnett, Joseph Bottum, Richard A. Epstein, Jacob Heilbrunn, Mark C. Henrie, Tod Lindberg